EASY ORIGAMI Kawaii

400 PAGES READY TO FOLD WITH 10 STEP-BY-STEP TUTORIALS

Kamikey

DAVID & CHARLES
—PUBLISHING—

www.davidandcharles.com

A DAVID AND CHARLES BOOK

David and Charles is an imprint of
David and Charles, Ltd, Suite A, Tourism House,
Pynes Hill, Exeter, EX2 5WS

Conceived, edited, and designed by Quarto Publishing,
an imprint of The Quarto Group, 1 Triptych Place,
London, SE1 9SH

First published in the UK and USA in 2025

A catalogue record for this book is available from the British Library.

ISBN-13: 9781446315866 paperback

This book has been printed on paper from approved suppliers and made from pulp from sustainable sources.

Printed in China.

10 9 8 7 6 5 4 3 2

Editorial assistant: Elinor Ward
Copy editor: Katie Hardwicke
Art director: Martina Calvio
Photographer: Nicki Dowey
Designer: Sally Bond
Managing editor: Emma Harverson
Publisher: Lorraine Dickey

David and Charles publishes high-quality books on a wide range of subjects. For more information visit www.davidandcharles.com.

Share your makes with us on social media using #dandcbooks and follow us on Facebook and Instagram by searching for @dandcbooks.

PAPER PATTERN CREDITS: AbraSa/Shutterstock.com; Agafonov Oleg/Shutterstock.com; AHMAD HIDAYAT RANGKUTI/Shutterstock.com; Anastasiia Gevko/Shutterstock.com; Anastasiia Guseva/Shutterstock.com; Anima Allegra/Shutterstock.com; Ann.and.Pen/Shutterstock.com; Anna Beatty/Shutterstock.com; antuanetto/Shutterstock.com; balwanrai/Shutterstock.com; burbura/Shutterstock.com; Byrka Ekaterina/Shutterstock.com; Chenspec/Shutterstock.com; claramh/Shutterstock.com; CS NoNo67/Shutterstock.com; Daniela Iga/Shutterstock.com; Dedraw Studio/Shutterstock.com; Dernkadel/Shutterstock.com; Don_ya/Shutterstock.com; ECE design/Shutterstock.com; Elena Emchuk/Shutterstock.com; Elizaveta Zaetes/Shutterstock.com; elysart/Shutterstock.com; FAST-Digimedia/Shutterstock.com; Foxelle Art/Shutterstock.com; GoodStudio/Shutterstock.com; Hanna Ilsv/Shutterstock.com; Innoria/Shutterstock.com; Irina Gorbunovair/Shutterstock.com; Jajojo/Shutterstock.com; KG_design/Shutterstock.com; Liliana Danila/Shutterstock.com; maradaisy/Shutterstock.com; Masha Minaeva/Shutterstock.com; Max Kohut/Shutterstock.com; Mint and Chips/Shutterstock.com; moibalkon/Shutterstock.com; NatalyFox/Shutterstock.com; NatthaponG21/Shutterstock.com; Olgastocker/Shutterstock.com; ONLY DESIGNZ/Shutterstock.com; prateek1502/Shutterstock.com; Oteera/Shutterstock.com; Queen Arts/Shutterstock.com; SayanRoychowdhury/Shutterstock.com; Slanapotam/Shutterstock.com; Sleek Genius/Shutterstock.com; sunwart/Shutterstock.com; Tanya Shulga/Shutterstock.com; Tatiana Bezogluk/Shutterstock.com; Textile Art and designs/Shutterstock.com; tn-prints/Shutterstock.com; xnova/Shutterstock.com.

Contents

Introduction

Hello everyone! I'm Kamikey, an origami artist from Japan and the author of *Easy Origami Kawaii*. Have fun following the 10 step-by-step tutorials for cute, easy-to-fold animals and characters, all perfect for beginners. The 400 sheets of paper that make up the rest of the book mean you have everything you need to get started.

Once you've finished folding, try drawing sweet "kawaii" inspired faces, as well as scales for your fish, spots for your ladybugs, and more! With your creations now finished, you can get even more creative by transforming them into birthday and Valentine's Day cards, gift tags, or decorative garlands for your friends and family.

Happy folding!

Kamikey
カミキィ

THANK YOU
For you
Love
Happy Birthday!

Folds & Symbols

Before you get started, study the opposite page carefully. It sets out all the basic folds and symbols you need to know to make the cute origami creations in this book. Each fold and its movement are represented on the step-by-step illustrations by an arrow.

Especially during the first steps, make sure to fold accurately by aligning the corners and edges perfectly. If the initial fold is off, the rest will be too, so it is very important to fold precisely from the beginning.

Another thing to remember is that dark colors, like black or brown, can make the crease lines harder to see, so for your first few attempts, it is best to use bright colors, like a light green or blue, which make the crease lines more visible.

If you find yourself stuck at any point, take a look at the next illustration and try moving the paper to match that shape. If you're not confident with drawing faces, try practising on a separate piece of paper first, or sketch with a pencil before committing to pen. Each project has three different facial expressions you could copy, but you can also get creative and experiment with your own.

Don't worry if your folds aren't perfect at first! The 400 sheets of paper will let you practise folding, unfolding, assembling and making any number of adorable creations.

Key:

Front
Reverse
Fold
Fold behind
Fold and unfold
Pleat fold
The dotted line shows where the paper will be.
Turn over
Open a gap
Next illustration enlarges
Cut

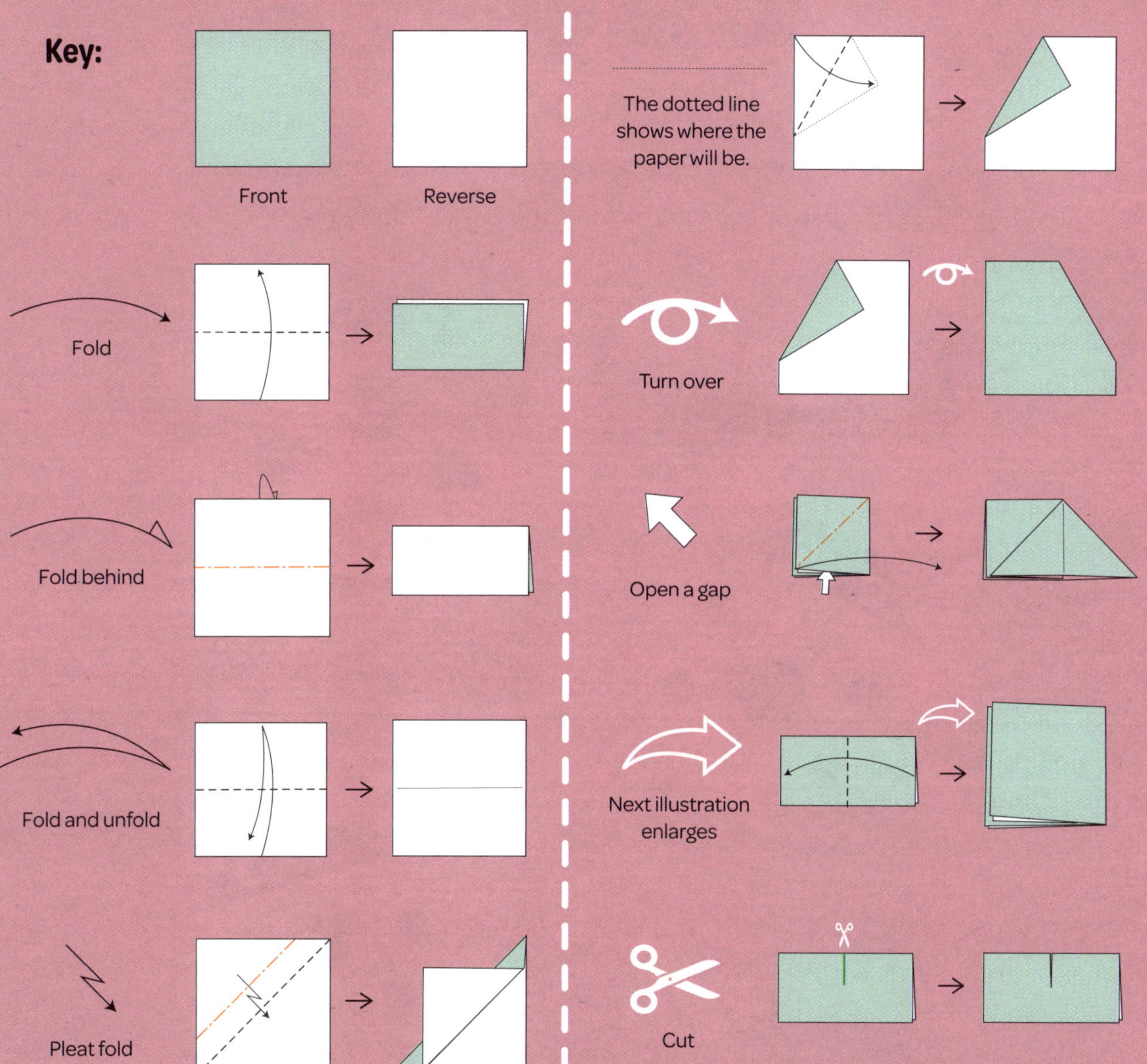

Ladybug

The simple steps make this ladybug perfect for beginners. Try making different ladybugs by changing colors and varying the number of spots on their backs.

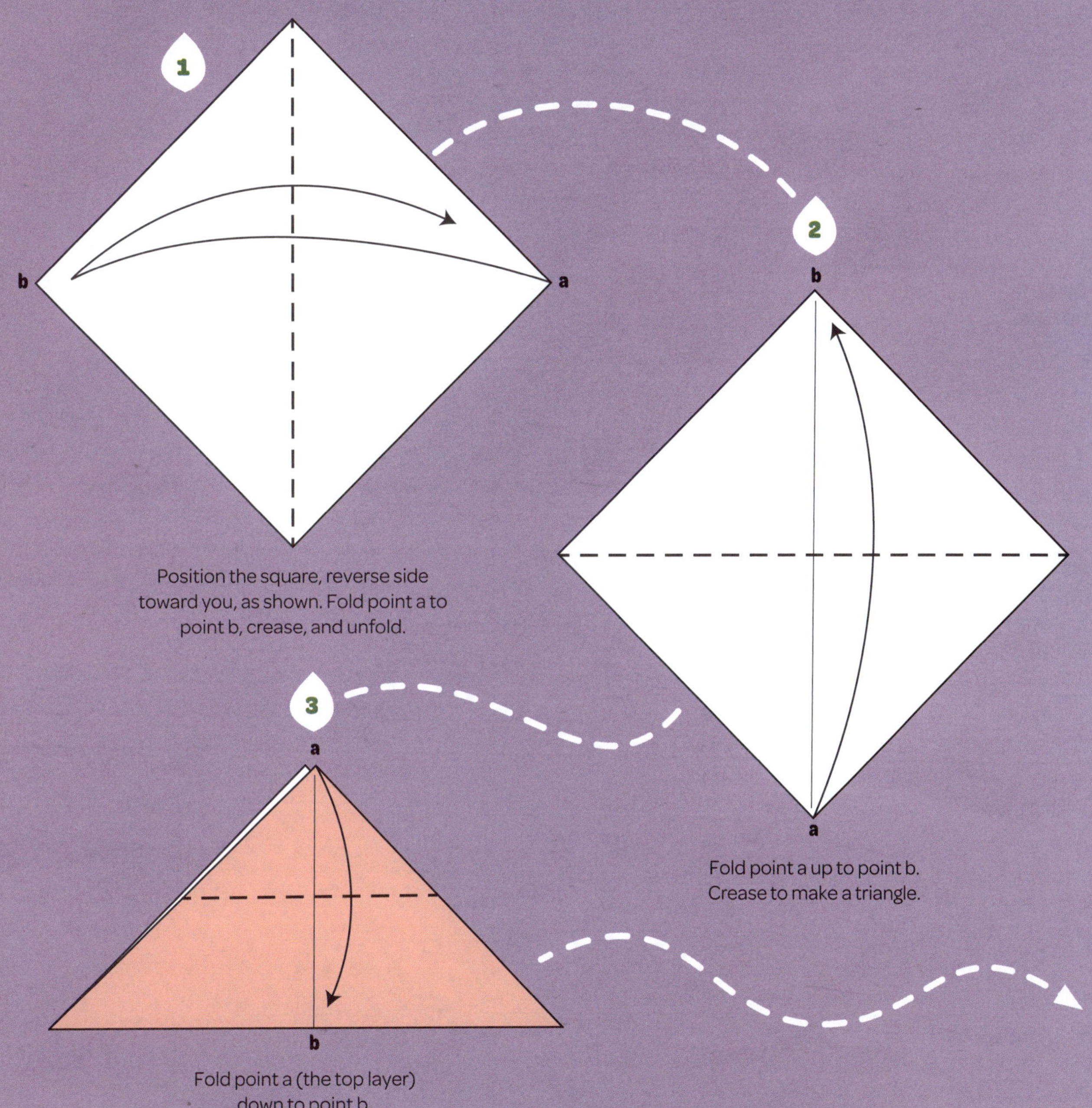

Position the square, reverse side toward you, as shown. Fold point a to point b, crease, and unfold.

Fold point a up to point b. Crease to make a triangle.

Fold point a (the top layer) down to point b.

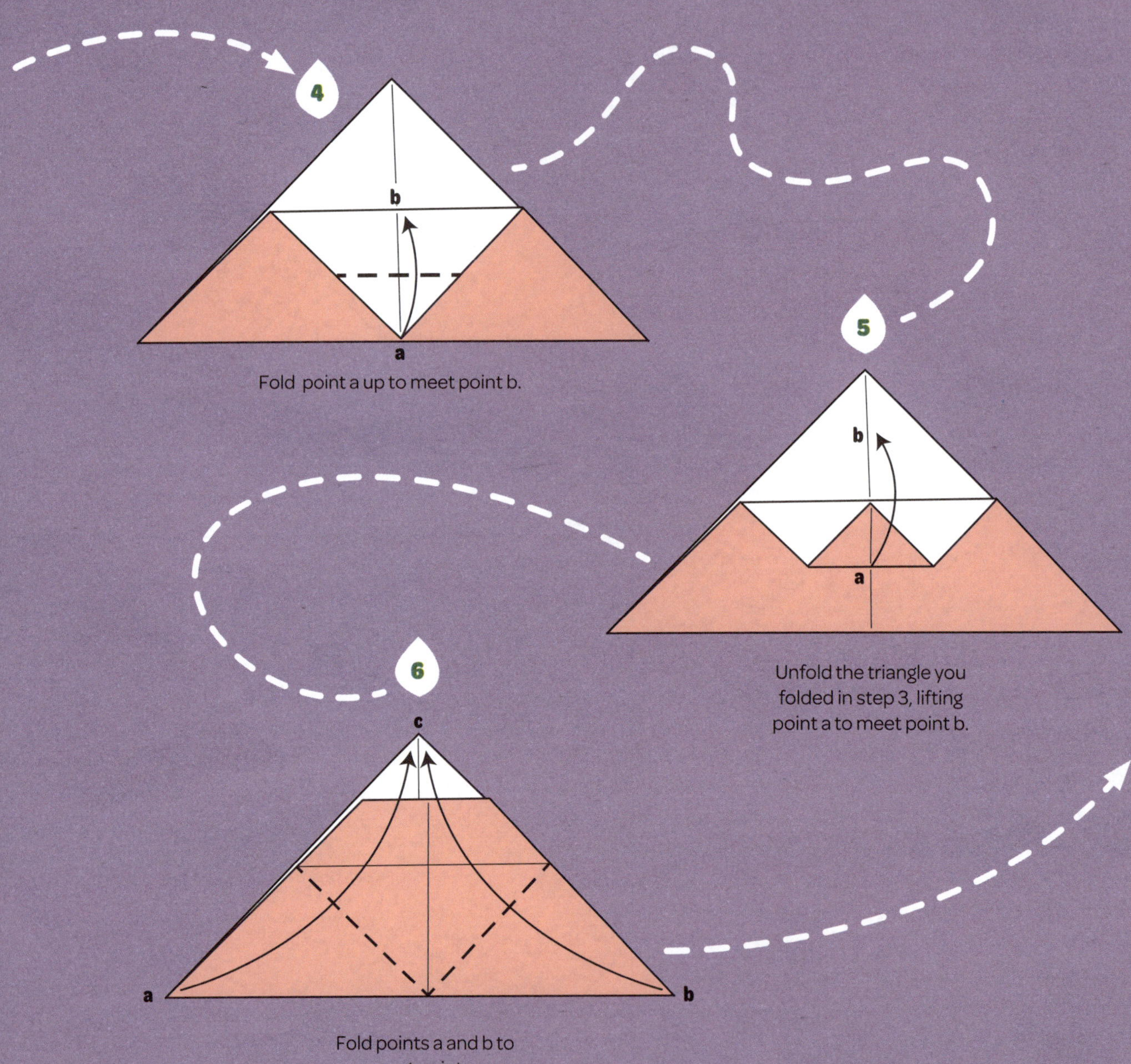

Fold point a up to meet point b.

Unfold the triangle you folded in step 3, lifting point a to meet point b.

Fold points a and b to meet point c.

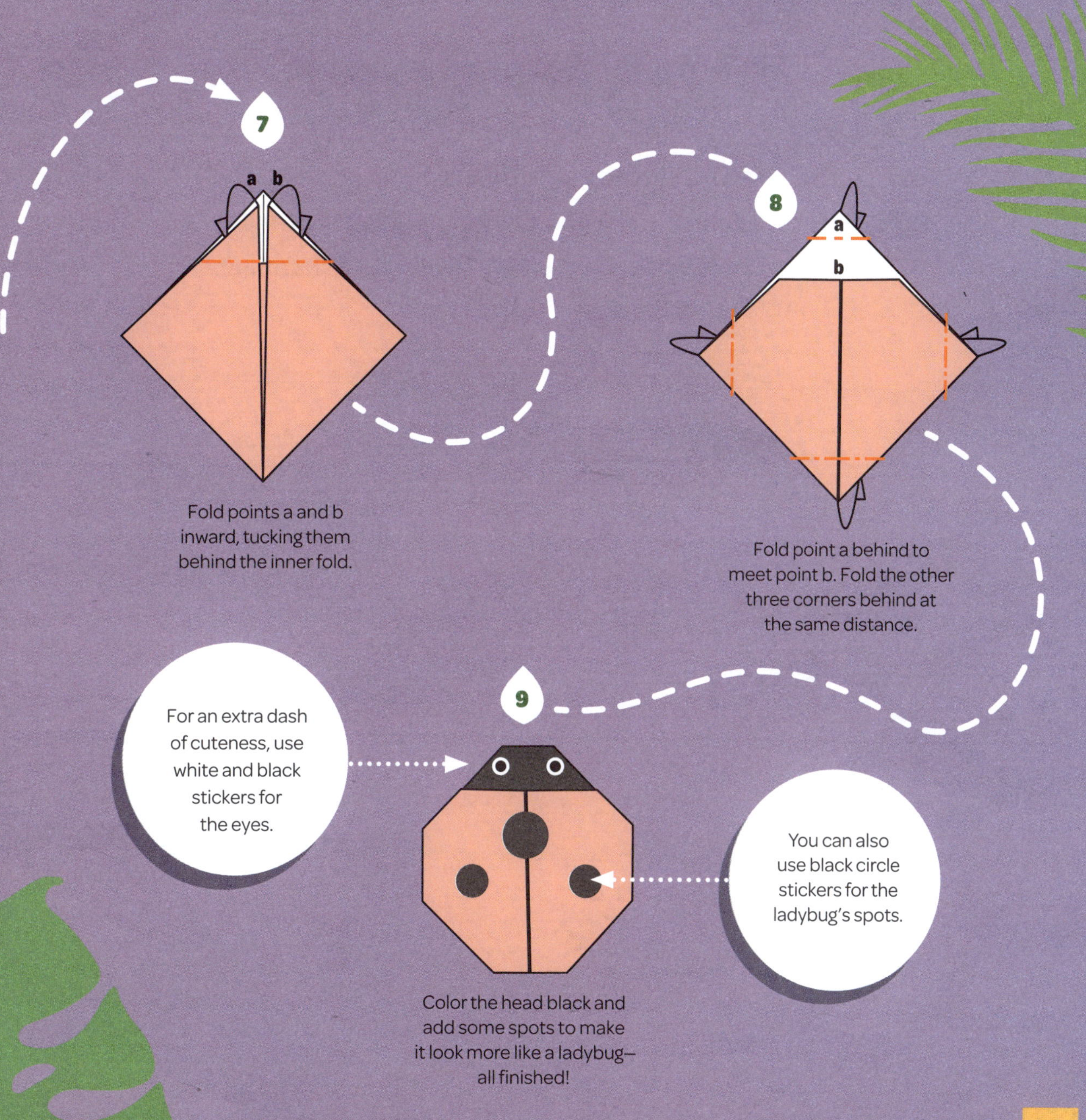
7
a
b
Fold points a and b inward, tucking them behind the inner fold.
8
a
b
Fold point a behind to meet point b. Fold the other three corners behind at the same distance.
9
For an extra dash of cuteness, use white and black stickers for the eyes.
You can also use black circle stickers for the ladybug's spots.
Color the head black and add some spots to make it look more like a ladybug—all finished!

Mushroom

Create a cute mushroom with these simple origami steps! It's easy to make and looks adorable with a drawn face. Using patterned paper will make it even more charming.

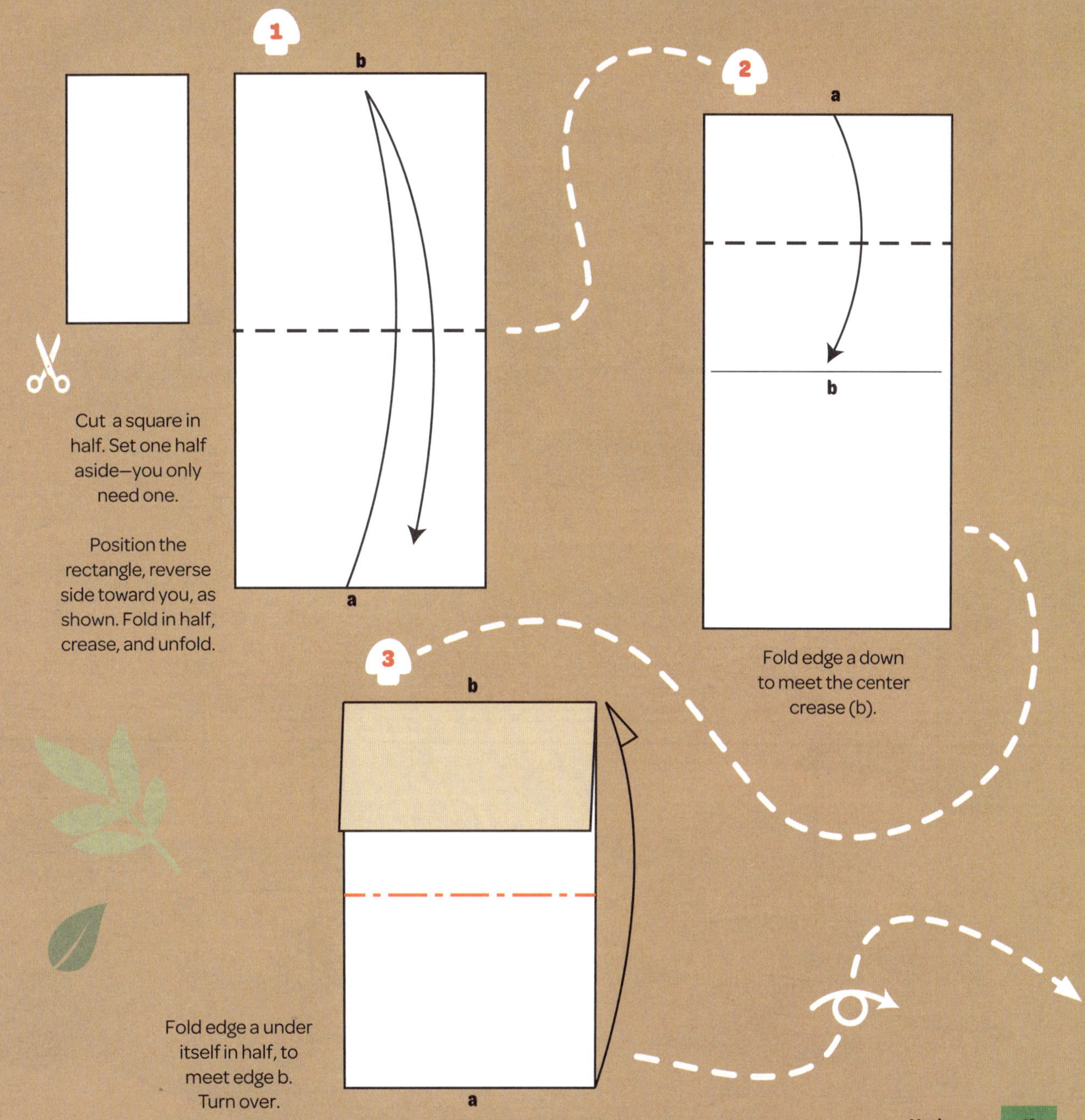

Cut a square in half. Set one half aside—you only need one.

Position the rectangle, reverse side toward you, as shown. Fold in half, crease, and unfold.

Fold edge a down to meet the center crease (b).

Fold edge a under itself in half, to meet edge b. Turn over.

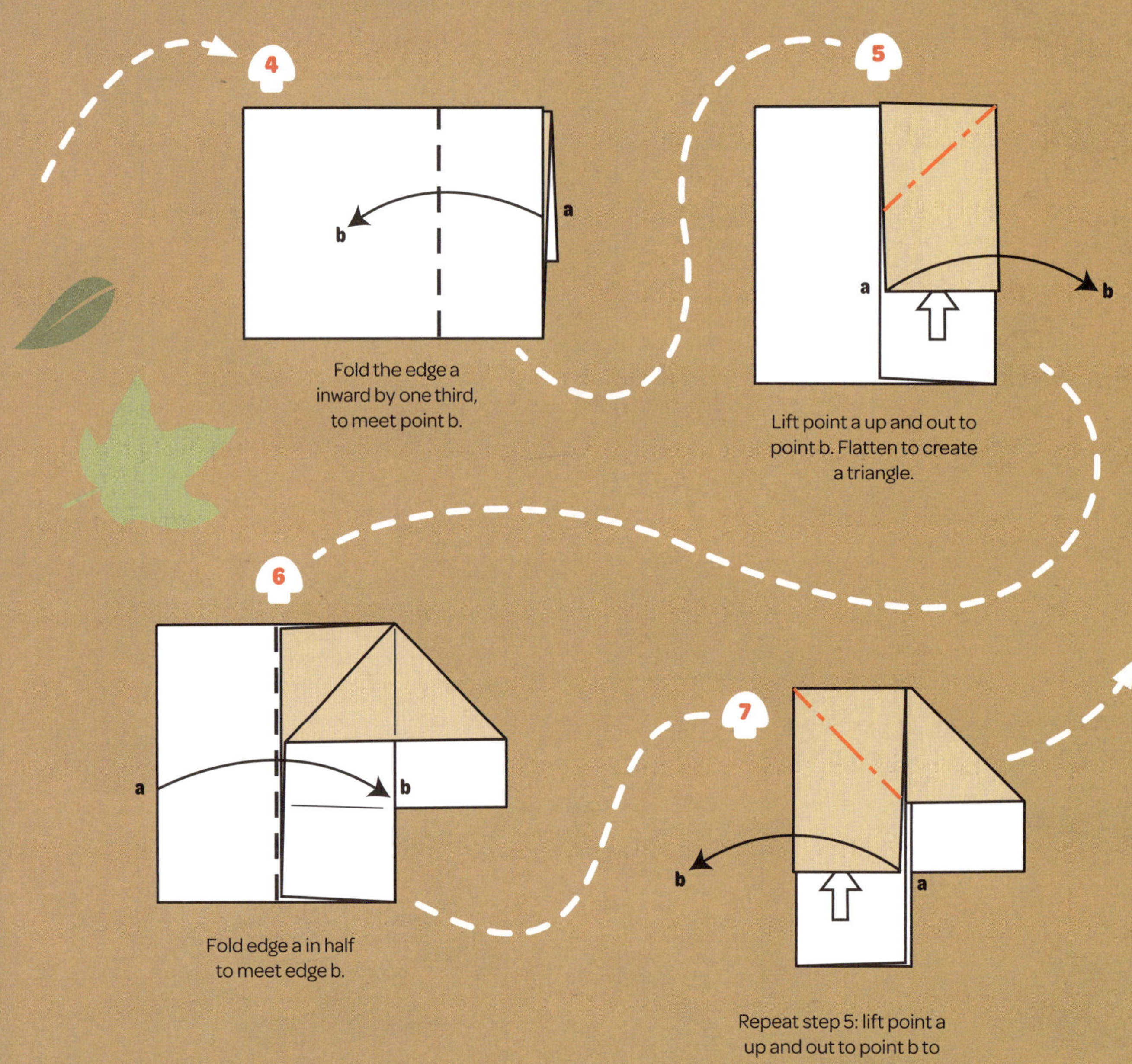

Fold the edge a inward by one third, to meet point b.

Lift point a up and out to point b. Flatten to create a triangle.

Fold edge a in half to meet edge b.

Repeat step 5: lift point a up and out to point b to create a triangle.

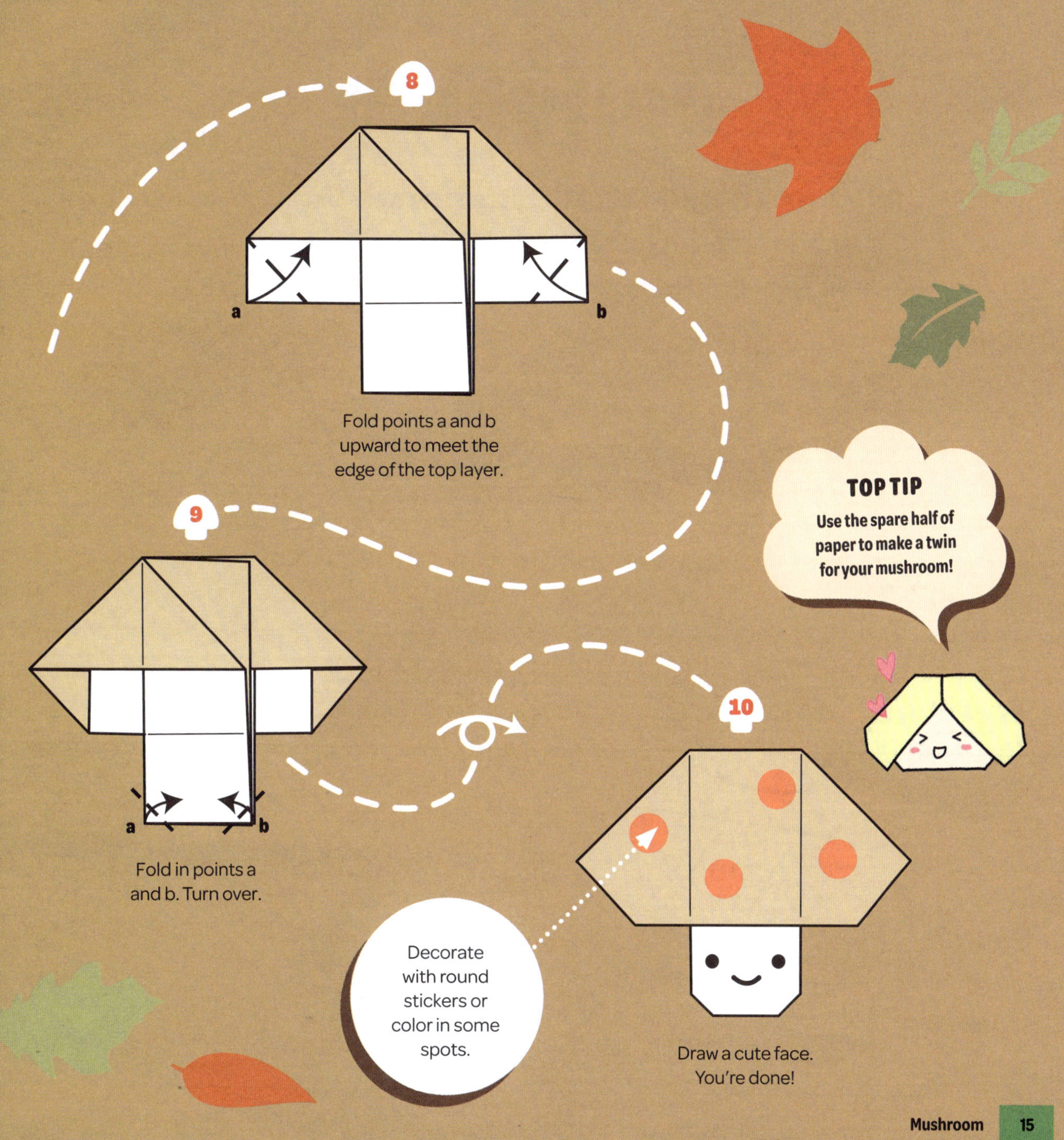
8
a
b
Fold points a and b upward to meet the edge of the top layer.
9
a
b
Fold in points a and b. Turn over.
10
Decorate with round stickers or color in some spots.
Draw a cute face. You're done!
TOP TIP
Use the spare half of paper to make a twin for your mushroom!

Jellyfish

Did you know that jellyfish are 95 percent water? Once completed, why not experiment with different facial expressions to capture the feeling of floating through a deep and endless ocean...

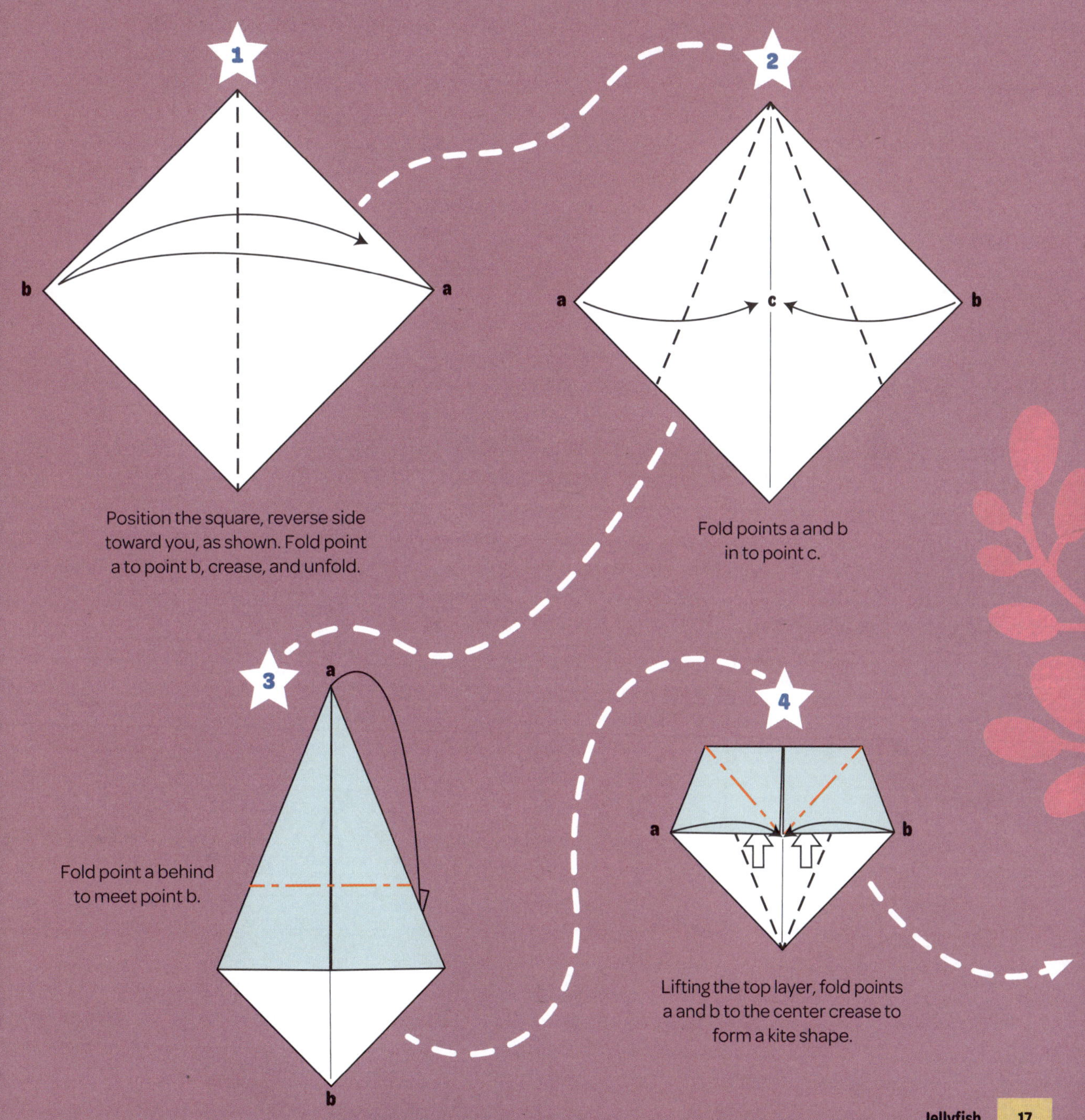
1
b
a
Position the square, reverse side toward you, as shown. Fold point a to point b, crease, and unfold.
2
a
c
b
Fold points a and b in to point c.
3
a
b
Fold point a behind to meet point b.
4
a
b
Lifting the top layer, fold points a and b to the center crease to form a kite shape.

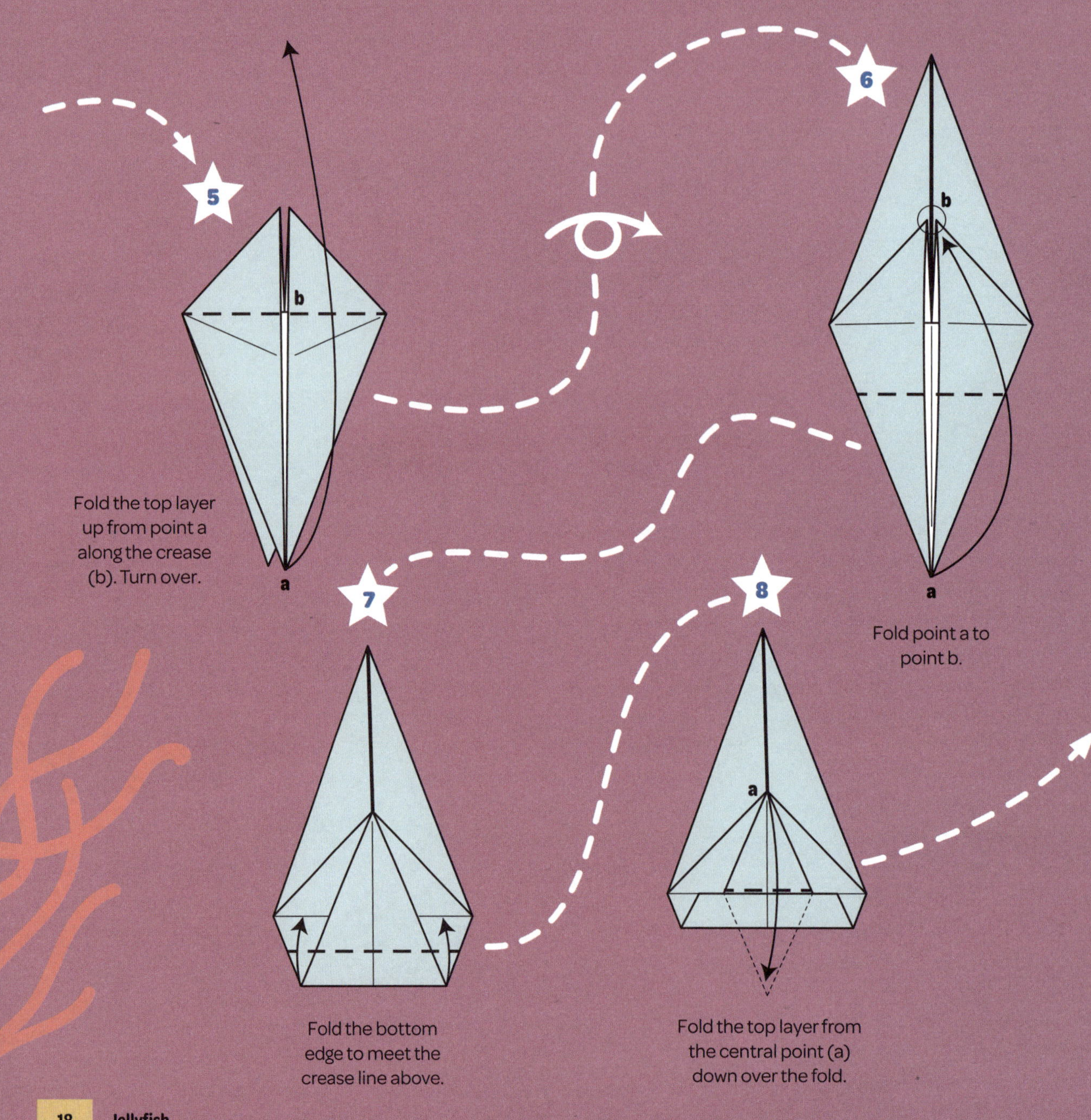
5
b
a
Fold the top layer up from point a along the crease (b). Turn over.
6
b
a
Fold point a to point b.
7
Fold the bottom edge to meet the crease line above.
8
a
Fold the top layer from the central point (a) down over the fold.

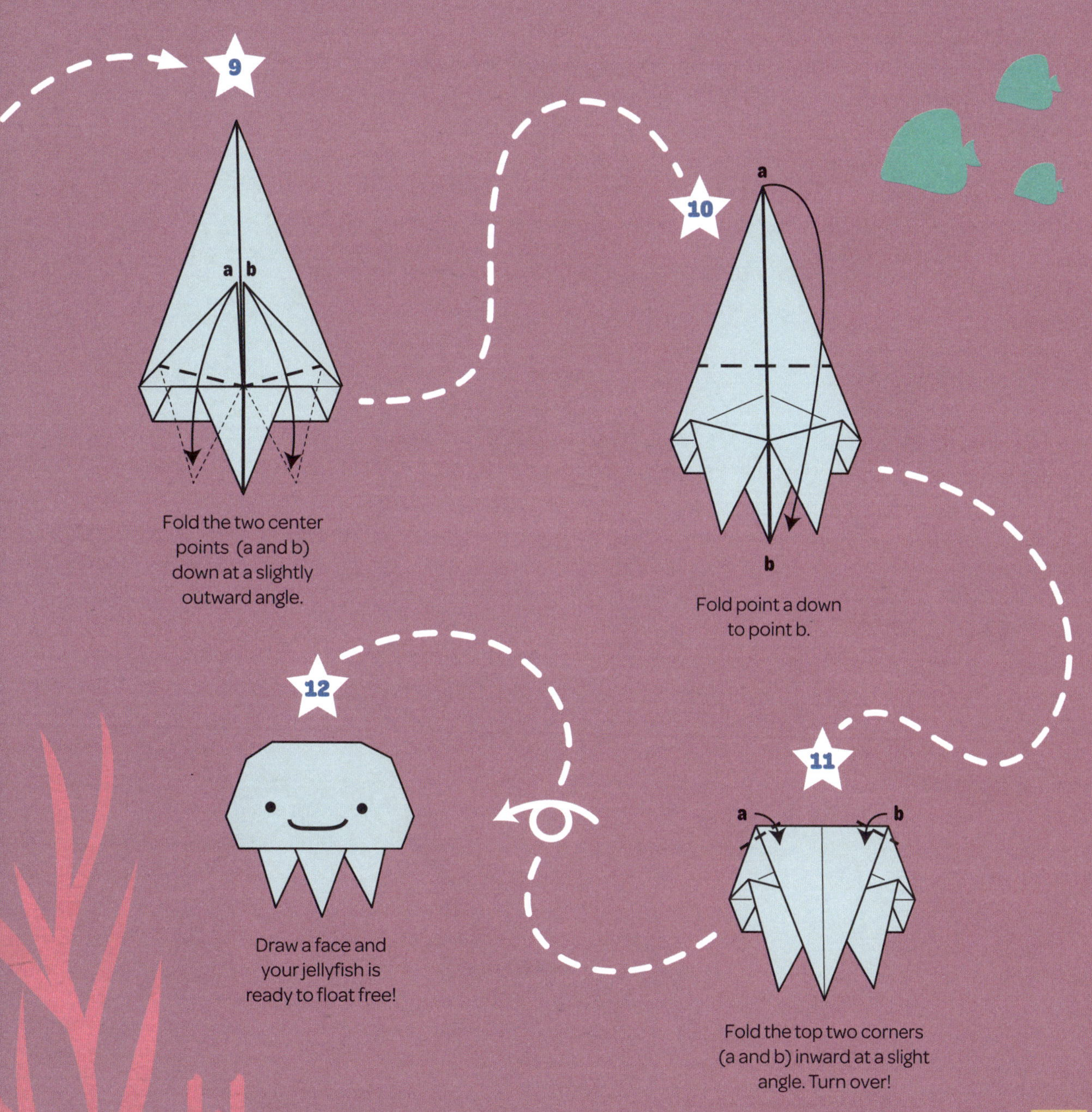

Fold the two center points (a and b) down at a slightly outward angle.

Fold point a down to point b.

Fold the top two corners (a and b) inward at a slight angle. Turn over!

Draw a face and your jellyfish is ready to float free!

Penguin

Create everyone's favorite penguin with this adorable origami design. You can personalize it by writing on its belly to turn it into a charming greetings card.

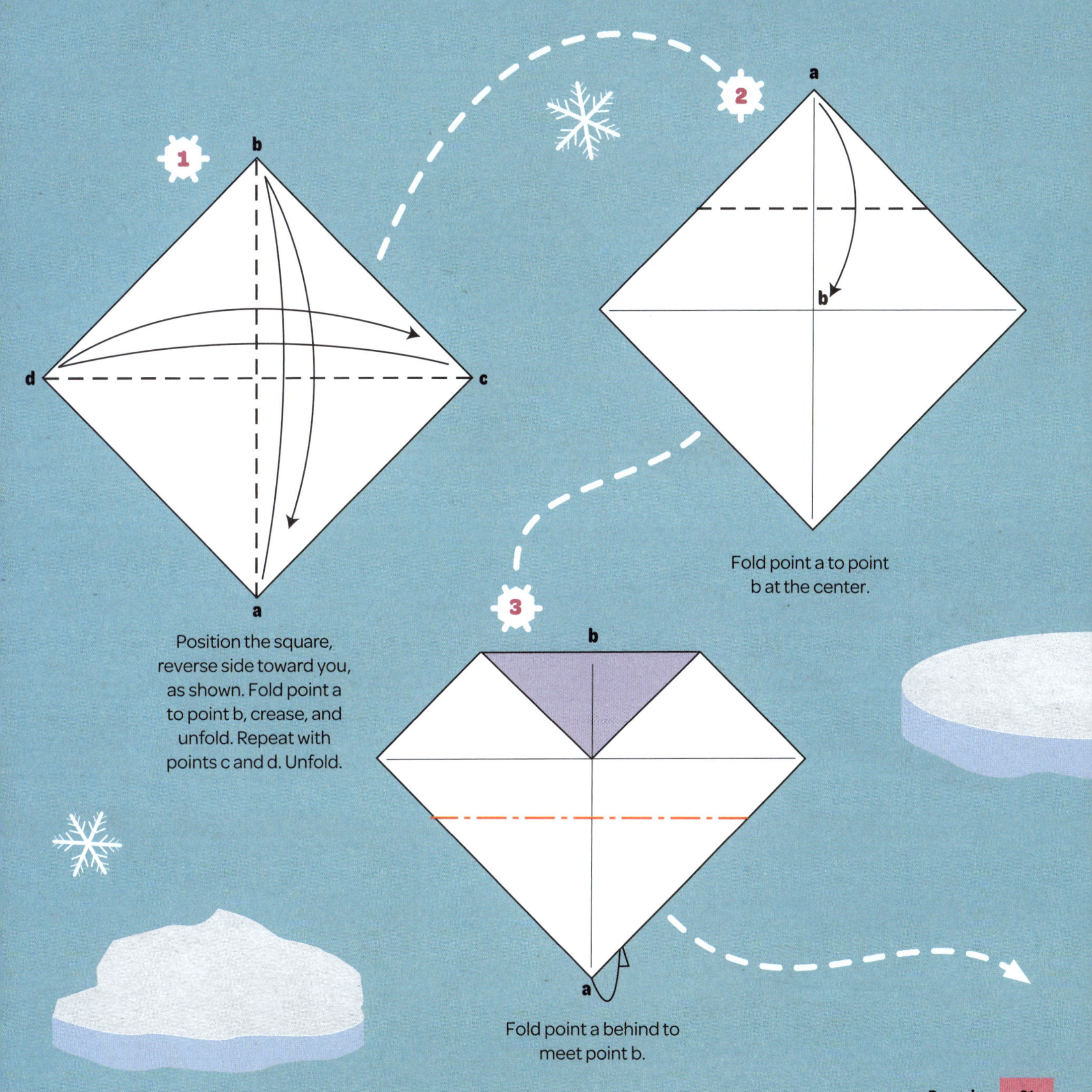
1
b
d
c
a
Position the square, reverse side toward you, as shown. Fold point a to point b, crease, and unfold. Repeat with points c and d. Unfold.
2
a
b
Fold point a to point b at the center.
3
b
a
Fold point a behind to meet point b.

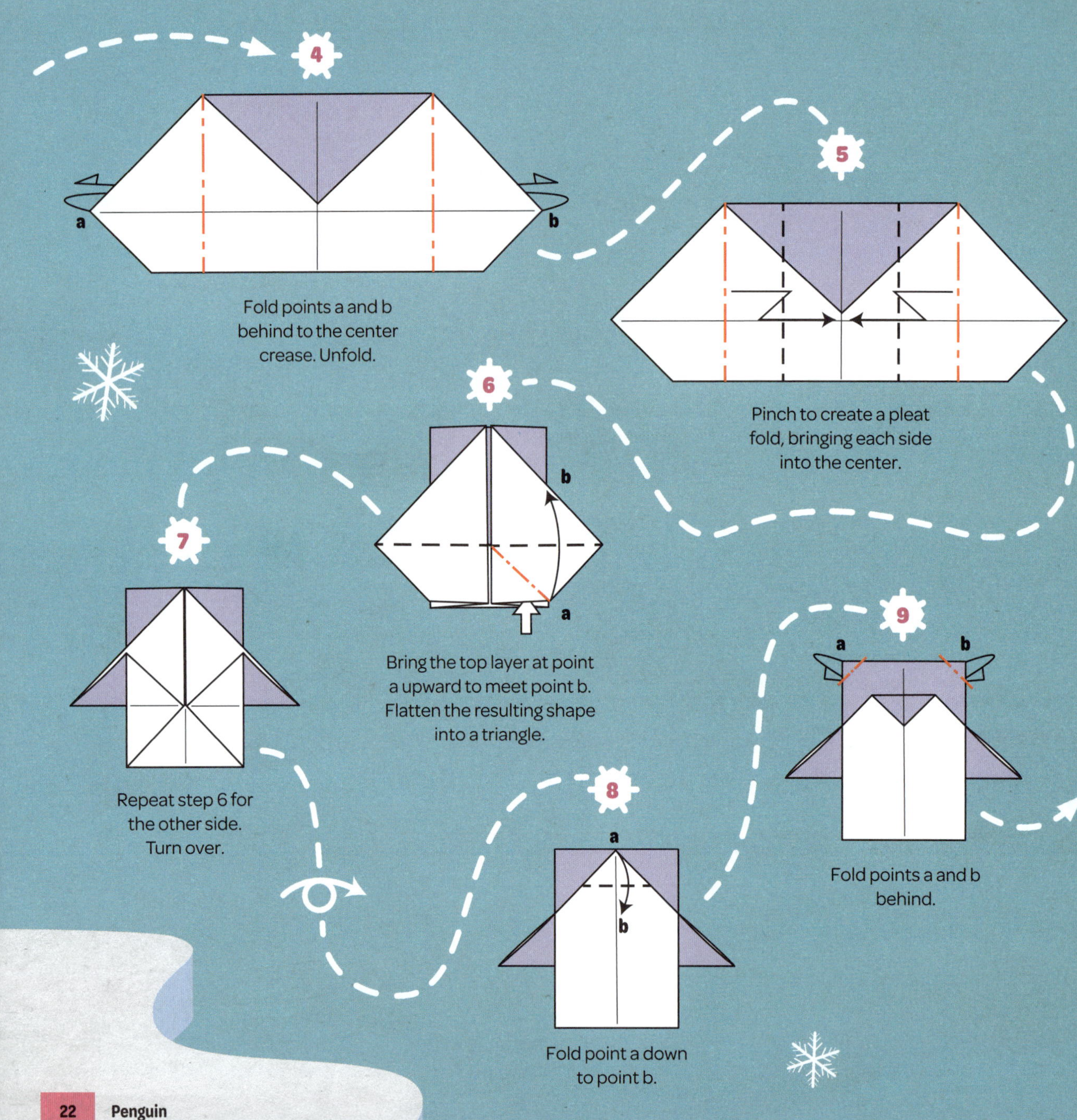
4
a
b
Fold points a and b behind to the center crease. Unfold.
5
Pinch to create a pleat fold, bringing each side into the center.
6
b
a
Bring the top layer at point a upward to meet point b. Flatten the resulting shape into a triangle.
7
Repeat step 6 for the other side. Turn over.
8
a
b
Fold point a down to point b.
9
a
b
Fold points a and b behind.

If you like, you can keep the arms outstretched by stopping here. Or, fold points a and b inward at a slight angle.

Add a pair of eyes. Your penguin is complete!

Fish

This is an easy-to-make fish, perfect for children and beginners. Get creative by adding intricate scale patterns to personalize your design or use a brightly patterned paper for a tropical touch!

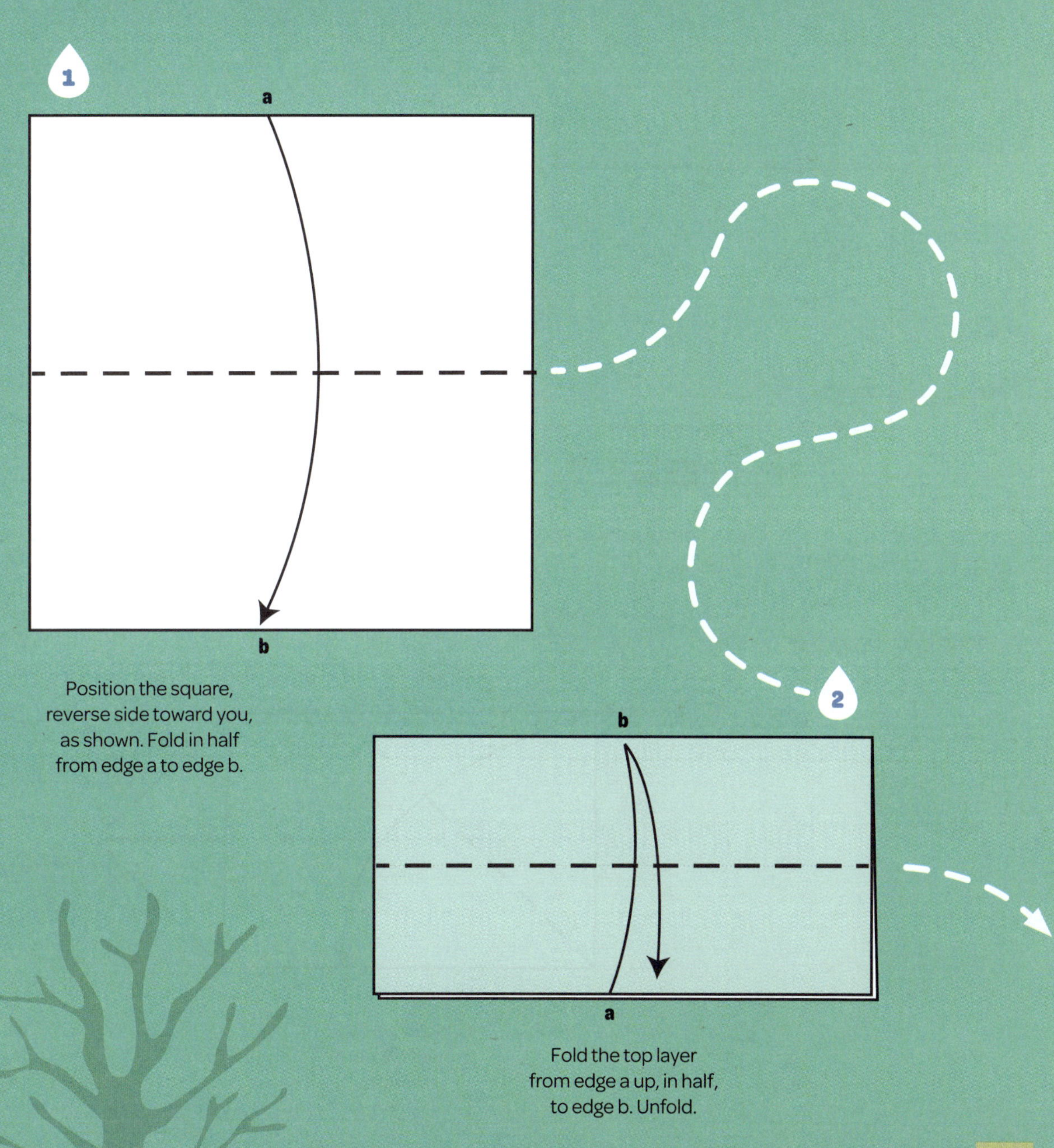

Position the square, reverse side toward you, as shown. Fold in half from edge a to edge b.

Fold the top layer from edge a up, in half, to edge b. Unfold.

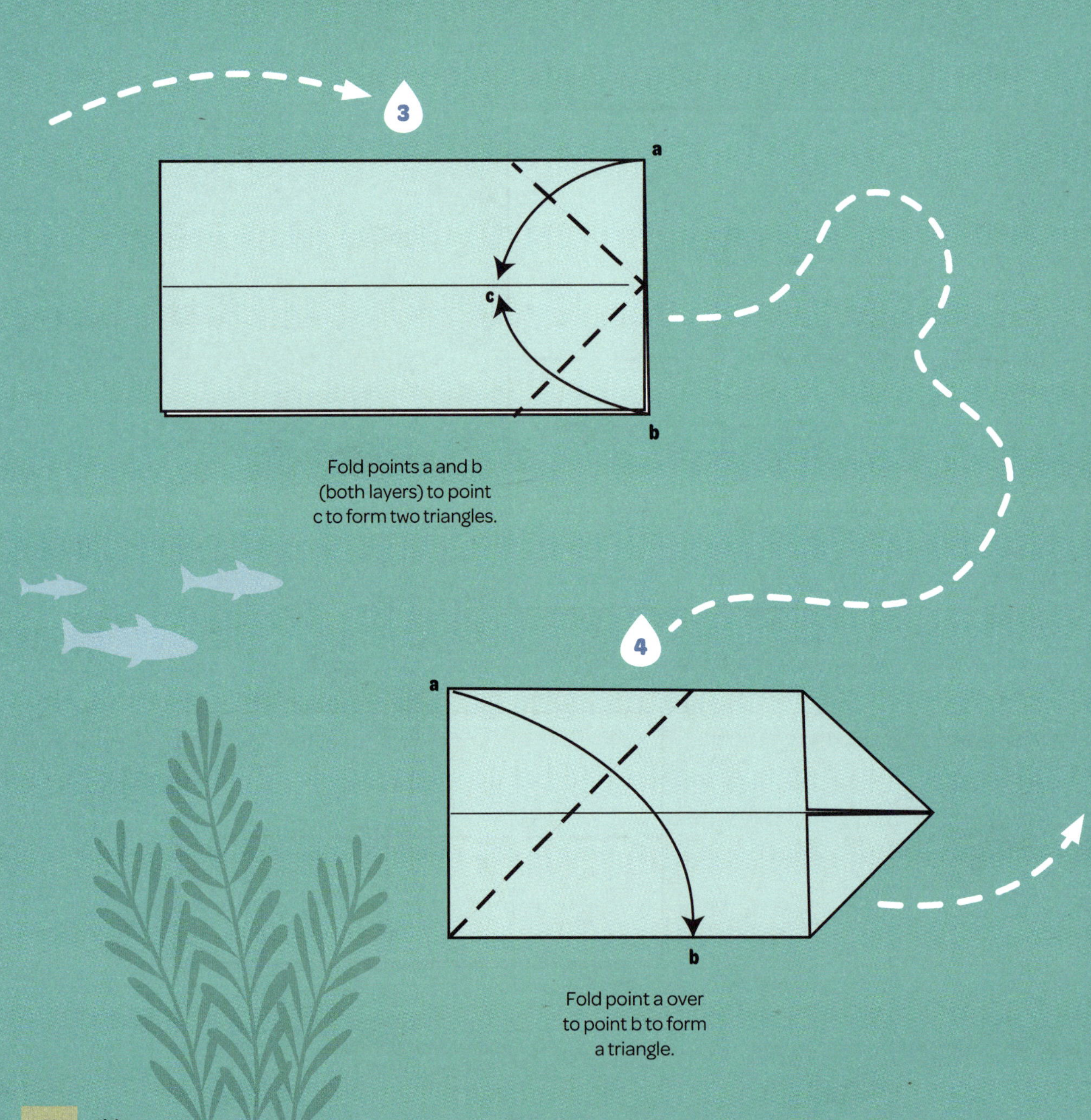

Fold points a and b (both layers) to point c to form two triangles.

Fold point a over to point b to form a triangle.

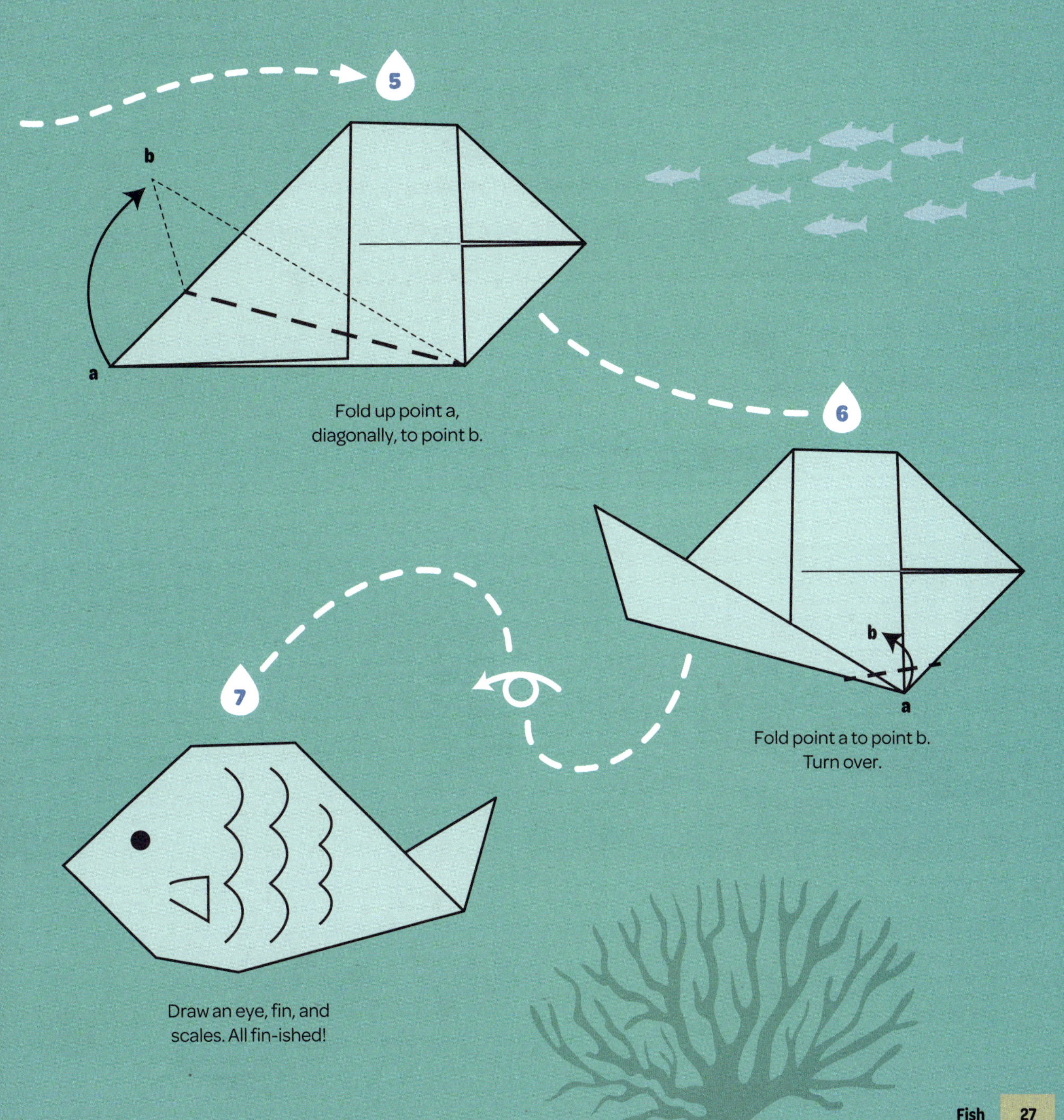
5
b
a
Fold up point a,
diagonally, to point b.
6
b
a
Fold point a to point b.
Turn over.
7
Draw an eye, fin, and
scales. All fin-ished!

Dog

Make this lovable origami puppy with floppy ears in just a few simple folds. Add a cute face to create an irresistible companion for any canine fan!

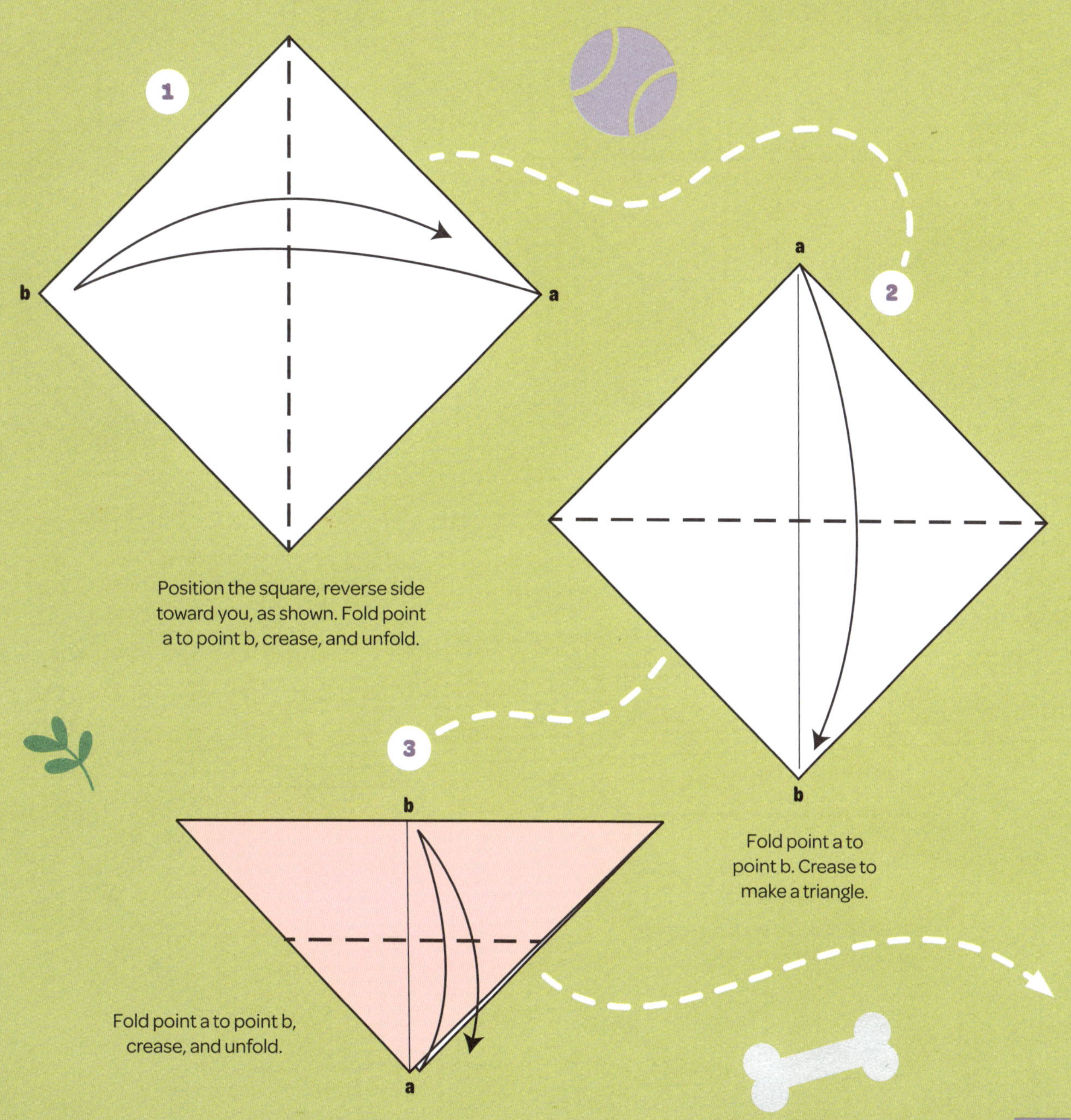
1
b
a
Position the square, reverse side toward you, as shown. Fold point a to point b, crease, and unfold.
a
2
b
Fold point a to point b. Crease to make a triangle.
3
b
a
Fold point a to point b, crease, and unfold.

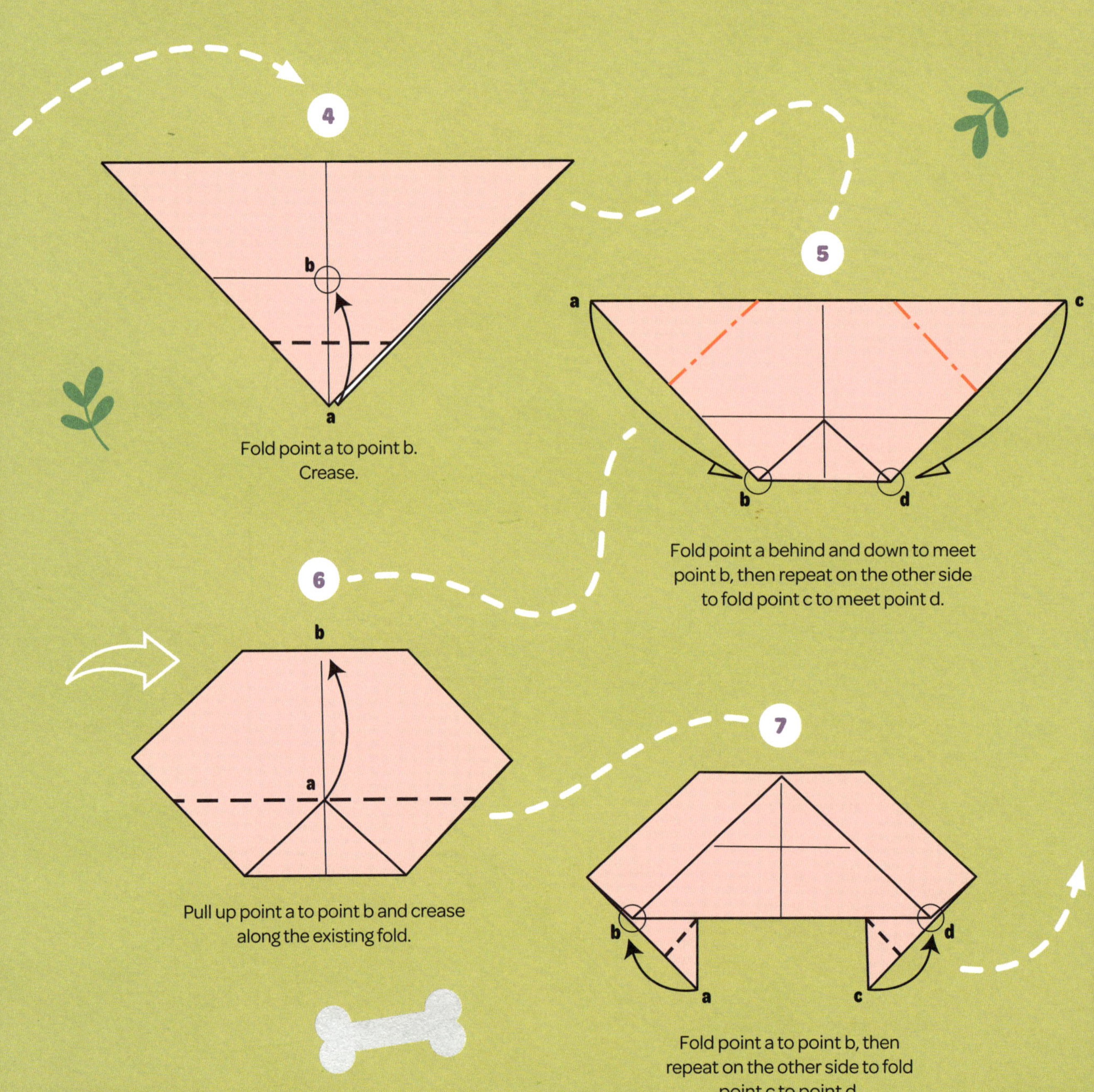

Fold point a to point b. Crease.

Fold point a behind and down to meet point b, then repeat on the other side to fold point c to meet point d.

Pull up point a to point b and crease along the existing fold.

Fold point a to point b, then repeat on the other side to fold point c to point d.

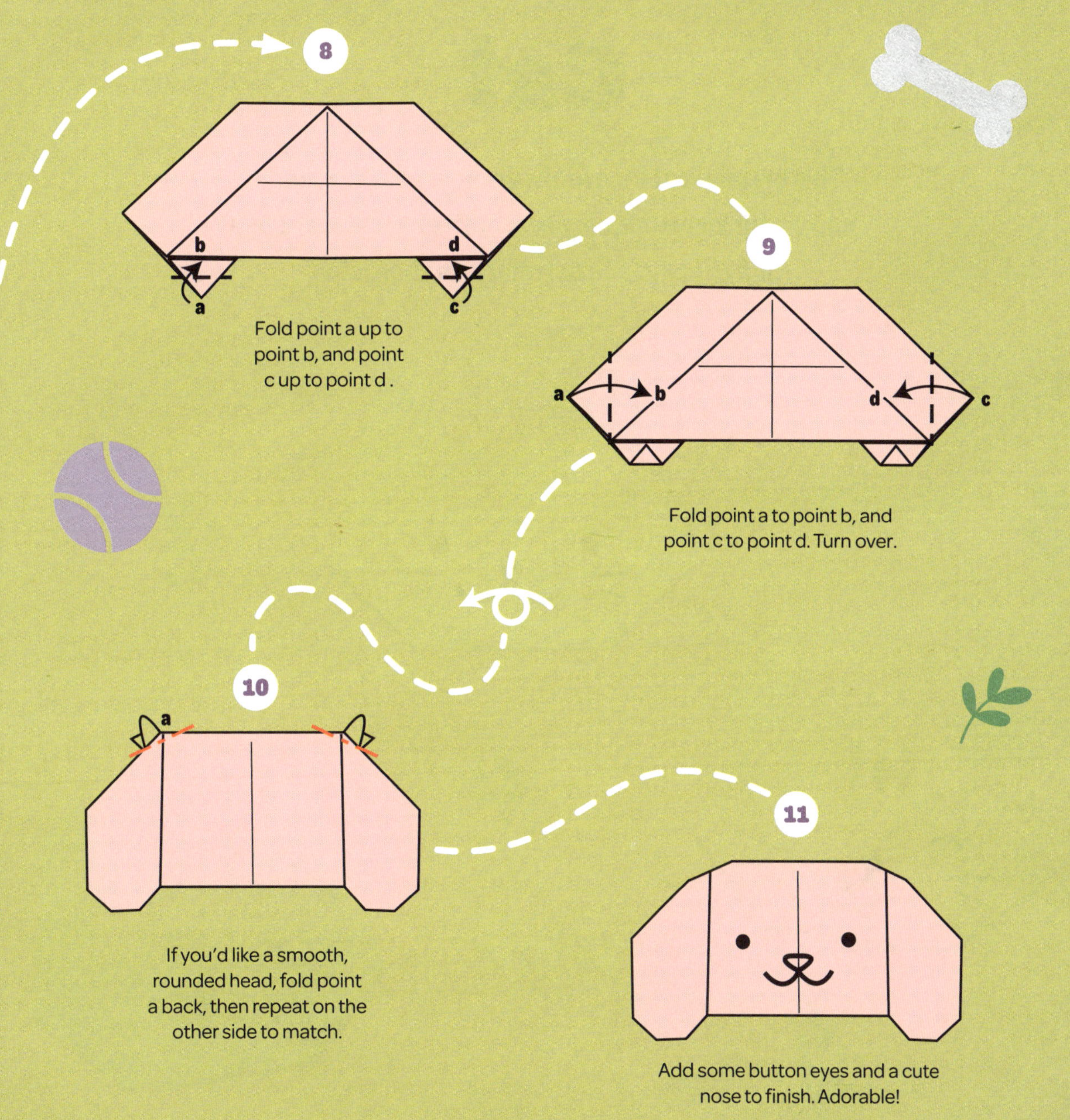
8
b
d
a
c
Fold point a up to point b, and point c up to point d .
9
a
b
d
c
Fold point a to point b, and point c to point d. Turn over.
10
a
If you'd like a smooth, rounded head, fold point a back, then repeat on the other side to match.
11
Add some button eyes and a cute nose to finish. Adorable!

Cat

This origami cat face looks great in solid colors. To make your kitty unique, personalize it with markings or a cheeky face to reflect its character.

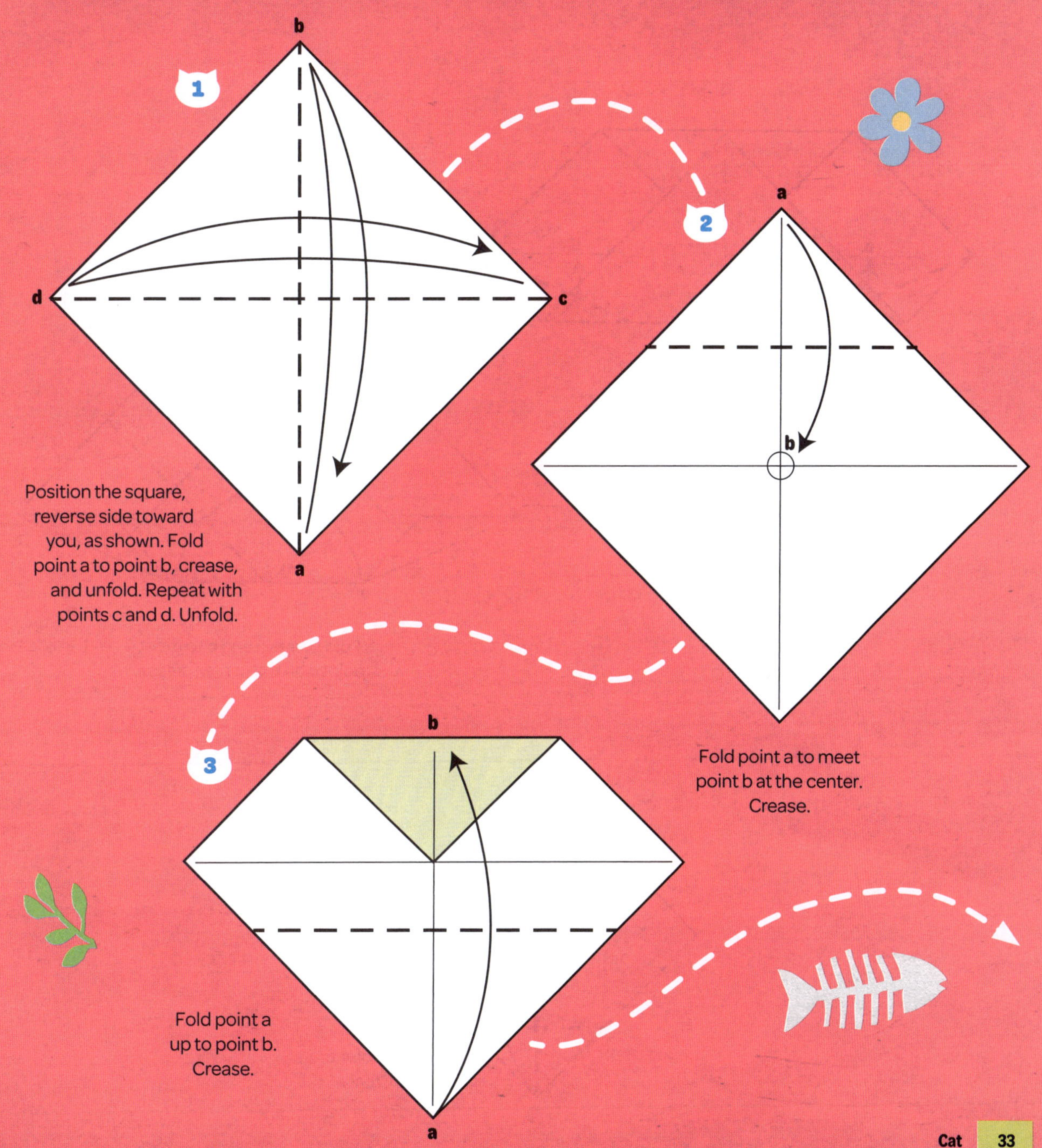

Position the square, reverse side toward you, as shown. Fold point a to point b, crease, and unfold. Repeat with points c and d. Unfold.

Fold point a to meet point b at the center. Crease.

Fold point a up to point b. Crease.

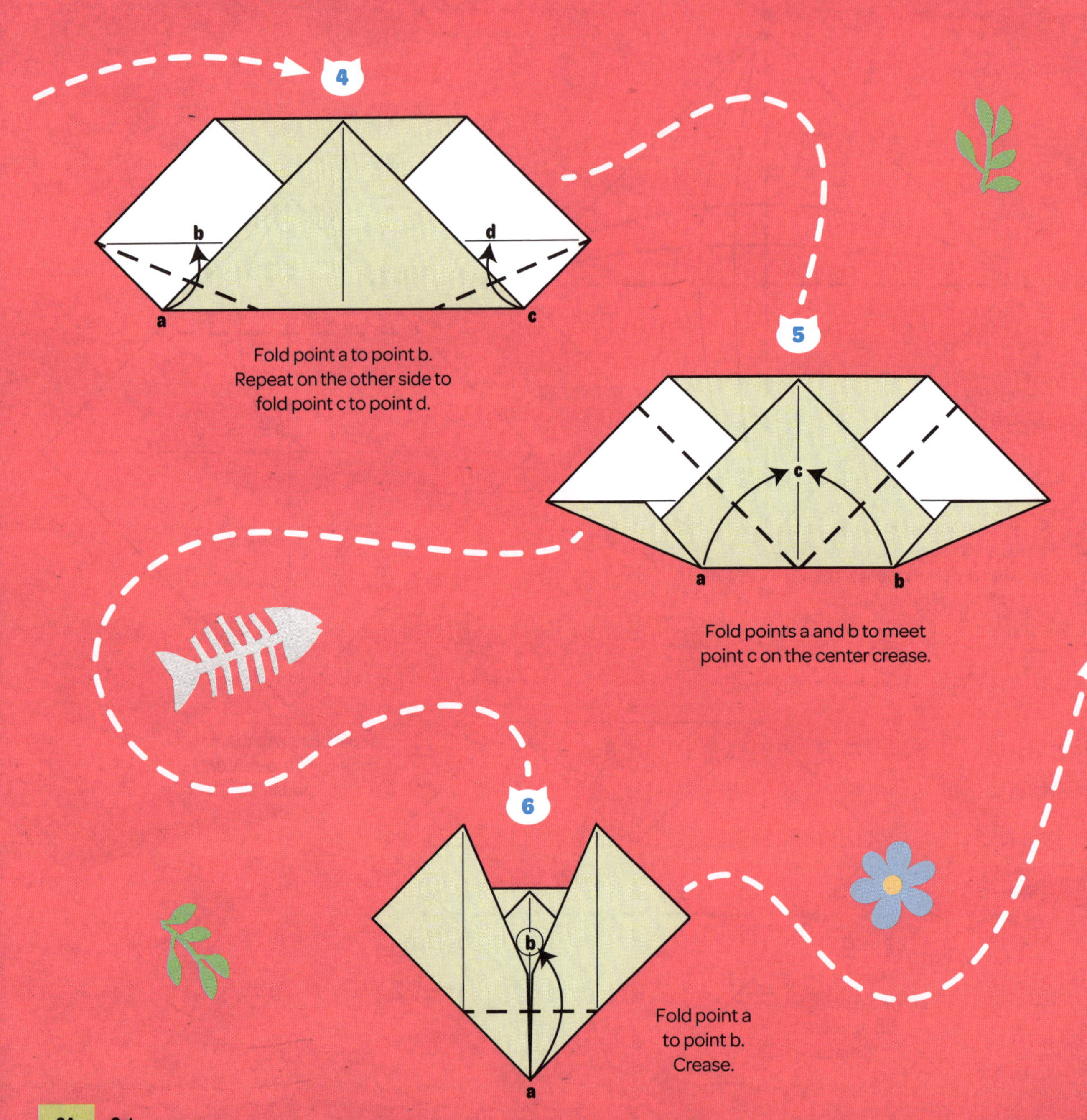
4
b
d
a
c
Fold point a to point b.
Repeat on the other side to
fold point c to point d.
5
c
a
b
Fold points a and b to meet
point c on the center crease.
6
b
a
Fold point a
to point b.
Crease.

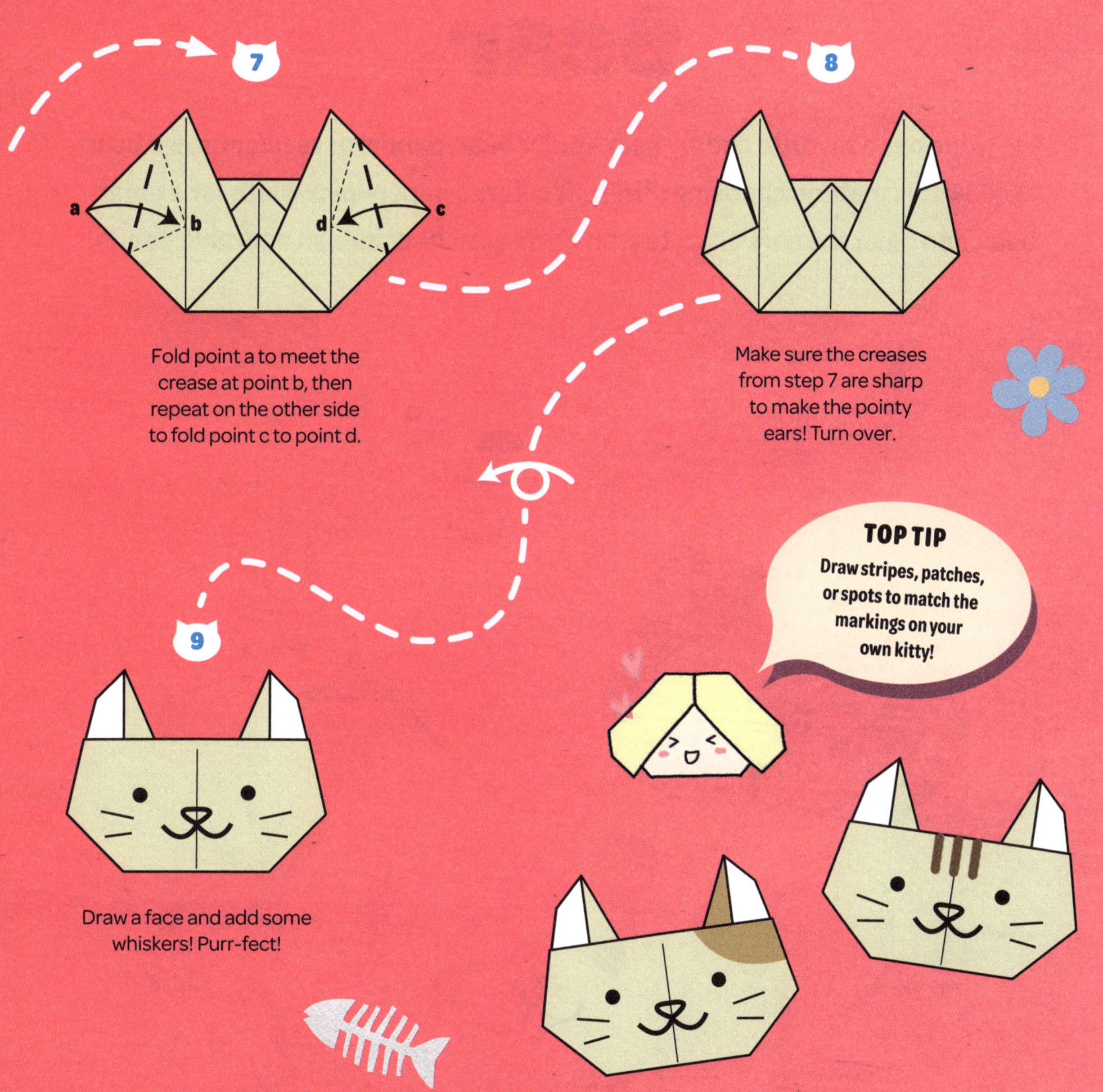

Fold point a to meet the crease at point b, then repeat on the other side to fold point c to point d.

Make sure the creases from step 7 are sharp to make the pointy ears! Turn over.

Draw a face and add some whiskers! Purr-fect!

Bear

Everyone has a favorite cuddly bear—polar bear, panda, or regular brown bear! Follow this method choosing different colored paper—pick white for a polar bear, and color the ears black to transform your bear into an adorable panda!

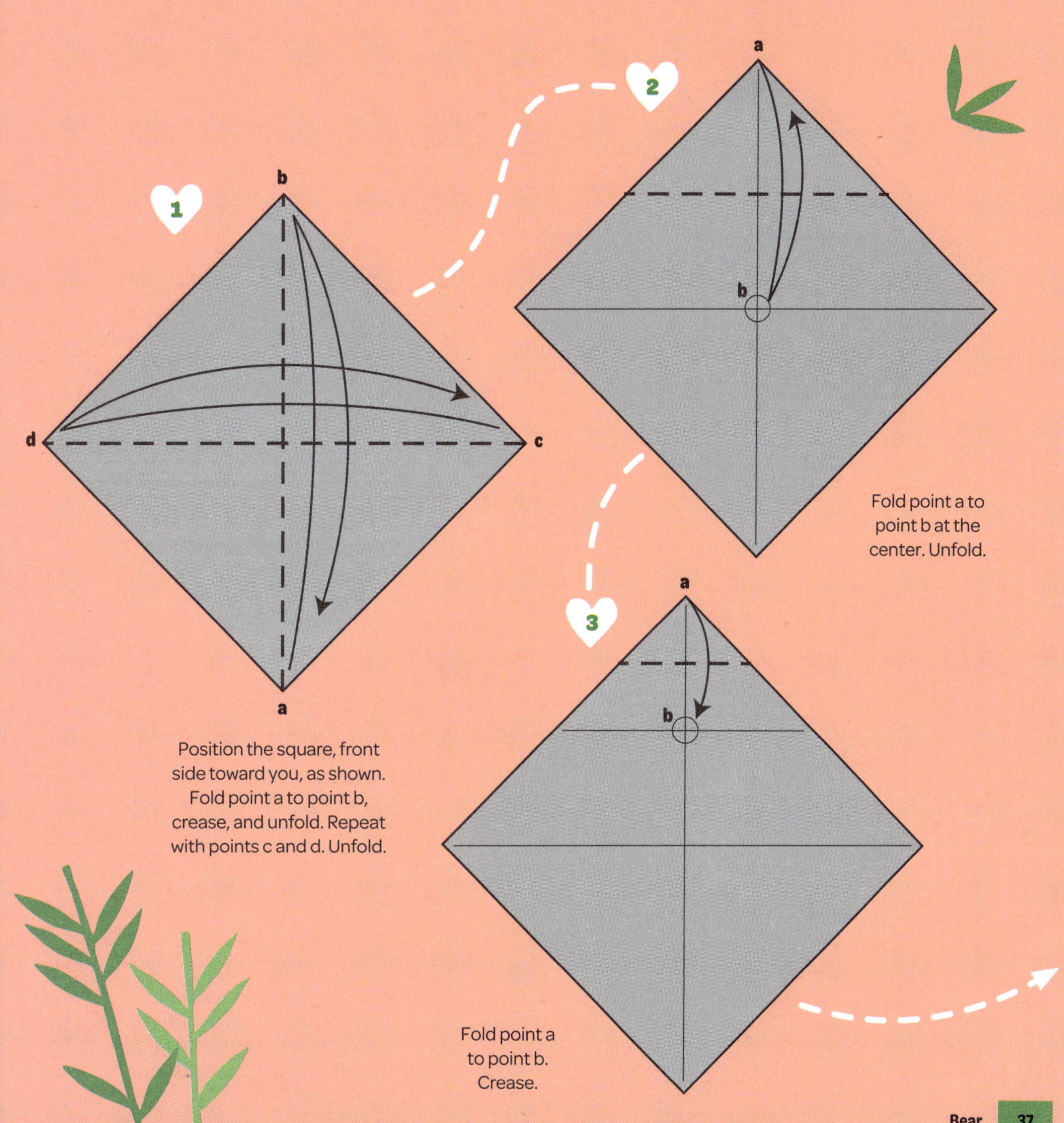

Position the square, front side toward you, as shown. Fold point a to point b, crease, and unfold. Repeat with points c and d. Unfold.

Fold point a to point b at the center. Unfold.

Fold point a to point b. Crease.

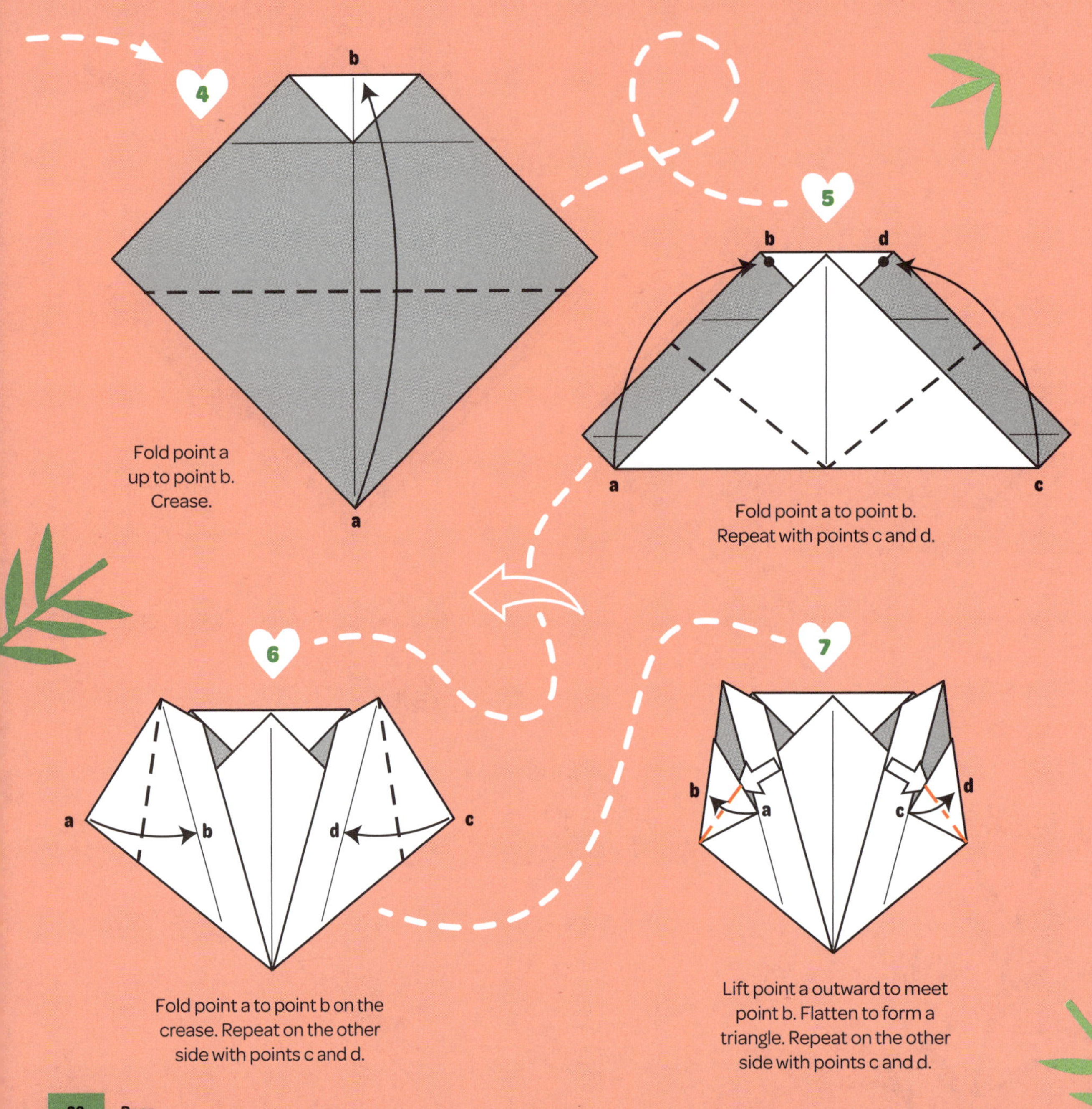

Fold point a up to point b. Crease.

Fold point a to point b. Repeat with points c and d.

Fold point a to point b on the crease. Repeat on the other side with points c and d.

Lift point a outward to meet point b. Flatten to form a triangle. Repeat on the other side with points c and d.

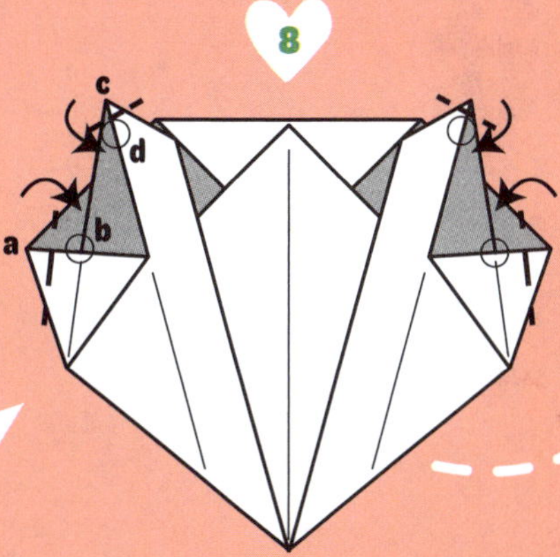

Fold point a to meet point b, and point c to point d. Repeat on the other side at the same distance.

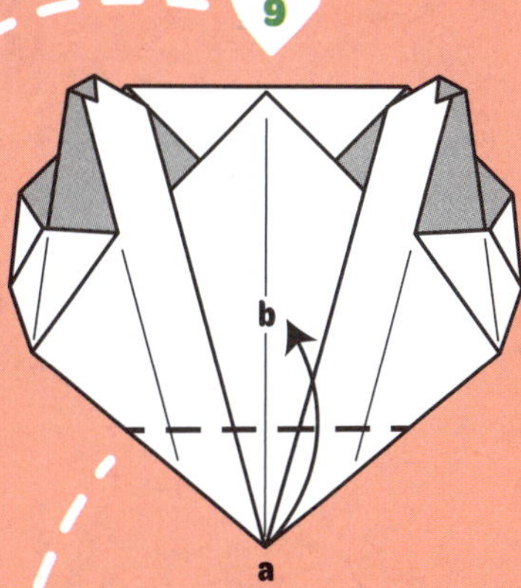

Fold point a up to point b. Turn over.

Draw a face using an oval shape for panda eyes. You're done!

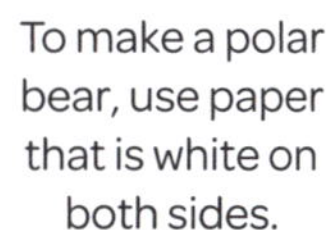

To make a polar bear, use paper that is white on both sides.

For a cuddly brown bear, use double-sided brown paper, or any solid color.

Rabbit

If you love rabbits, be sure to make this sweet origami! For a fun and easy project for all ages, why not make spring decorations by joining the bunnies together in a garland?

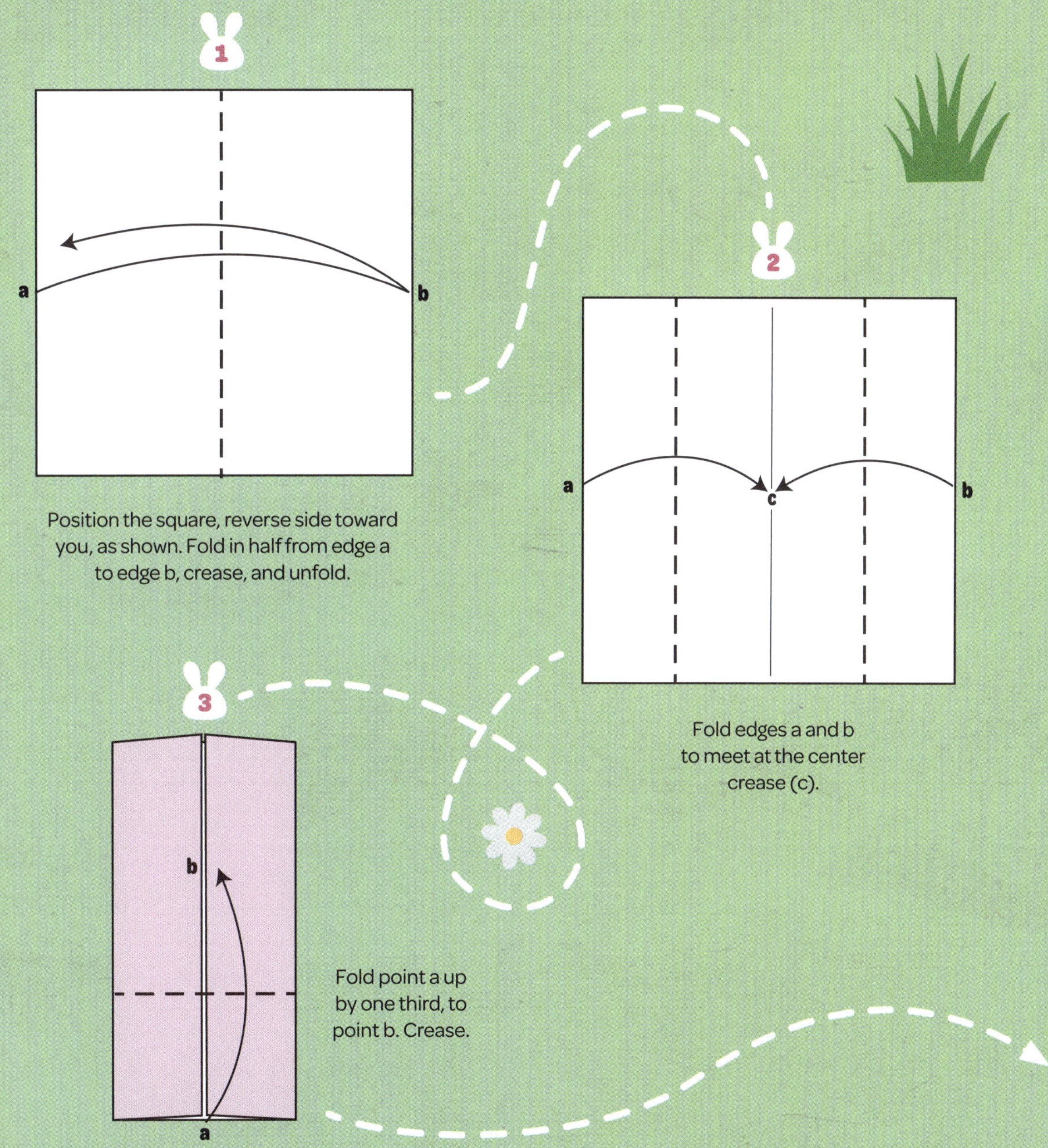

Position the square, reverse side toward you, as shown. Fold in half from edge a to edge b, crease, and unfold.

Fold edges a and b to meet at the center crease (c).

Fold point a up by one third, to point b. Crease.

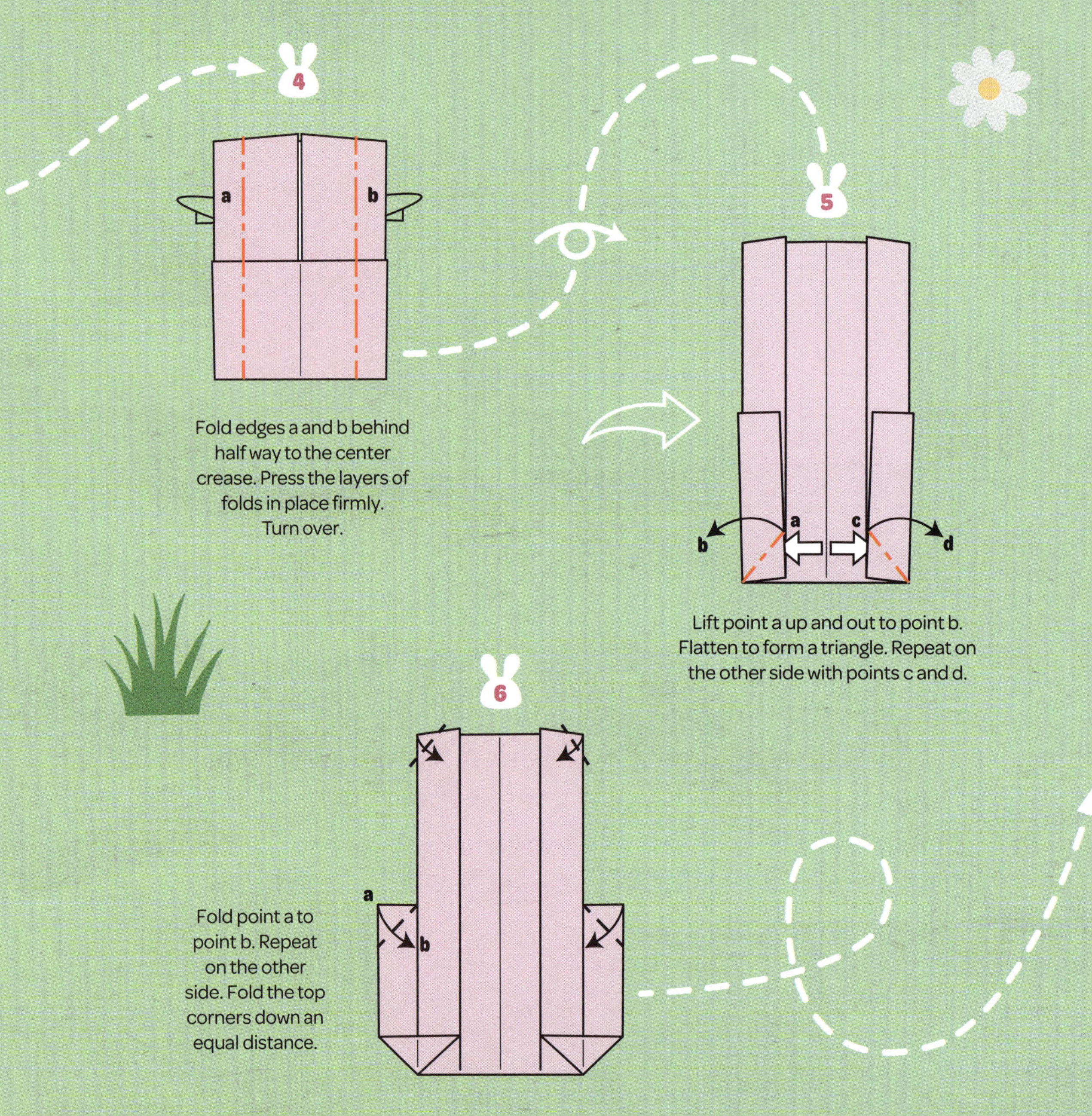

Fold edges a and b behind half way to the center crease. Press the layers of folds in place firmly. Turn over.

Lift point a up and out to point b. Flatten to form a triangle. Repeat on the other side with points c and d.

Fold point a to point b. Repeat on the other side. Fold the top corners down an equal distance.

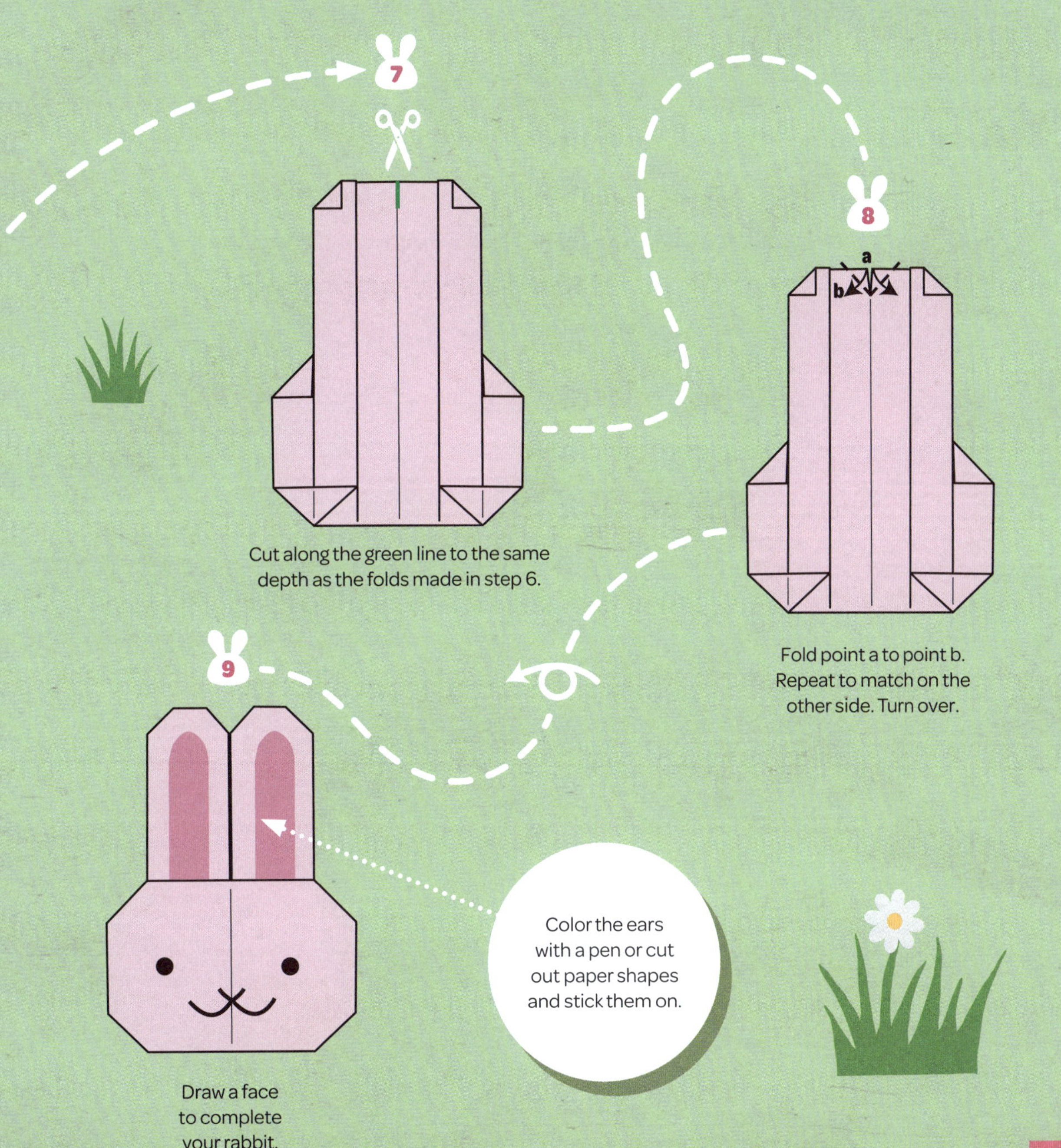

Cut along the green line to the same depth as the folds made in step 6.

Fold point a to point b. Repeat to match on the other side. Turn over.

Draw a face to complete your rabbit.

Color the ears with a pen or cut out paper shapes and stick them on.

Girl & Boy

Choose different hairstyles and body shapes to create cute origami girls and boys. For a fun variation, use patterned paper for the body—or the hair!

Bob hair

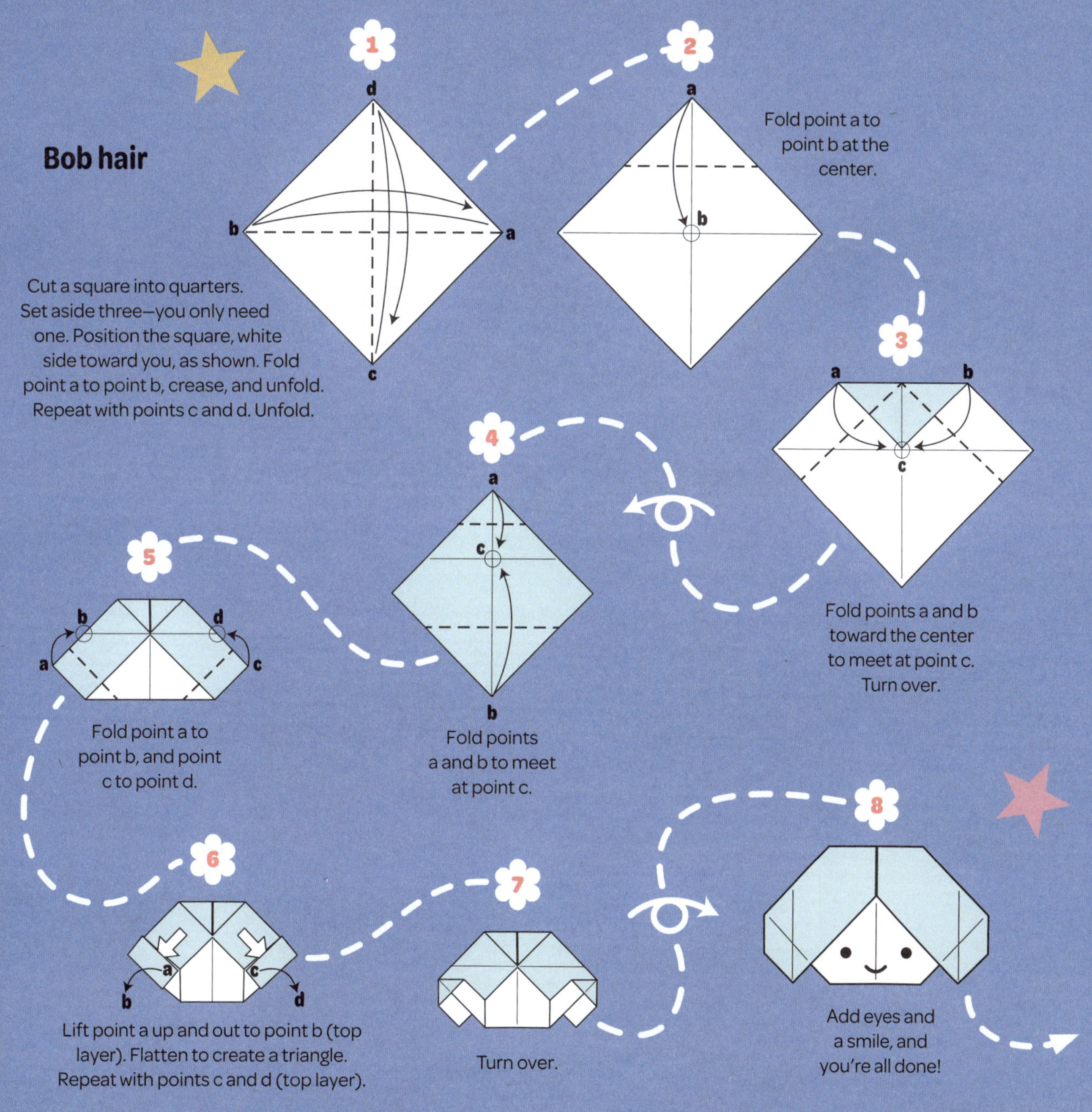

Cut a square into quarters. Set aside three—you only need one. Position the square, white side toward you, as shown. Fold point a to point b, crease, and unfold. Repeat with points c and d. Unfold.

Fold point a to point b at the center.

Fold points a and b toward the center to meet at point c. Turn over.

Fold points a and b to meet at point c.

Fold point a to point b, and point c to point d.

Lift point a up and out to point b (top layer). Flatten to create a triangle. Repeat with points c and d (top layer).

Turn over.

Add eyes and a smile, and you're all done!

Short hair

Follow steps 1 to 5 of the bob shape on page 45.

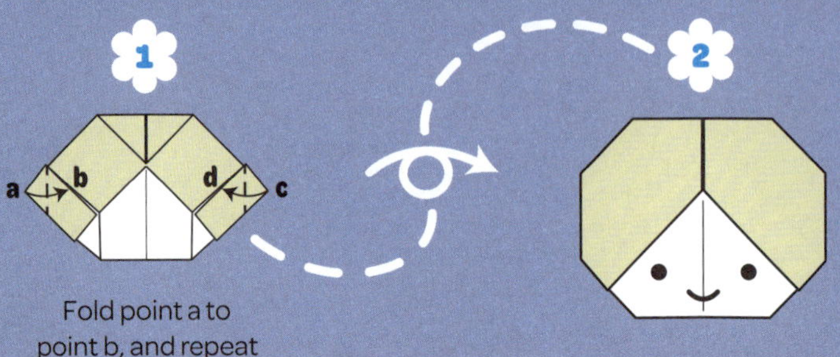

1. Fold point a to point b, and repeat with points c and d. Turn over.

2. Finish by drawing the face.

Long hair

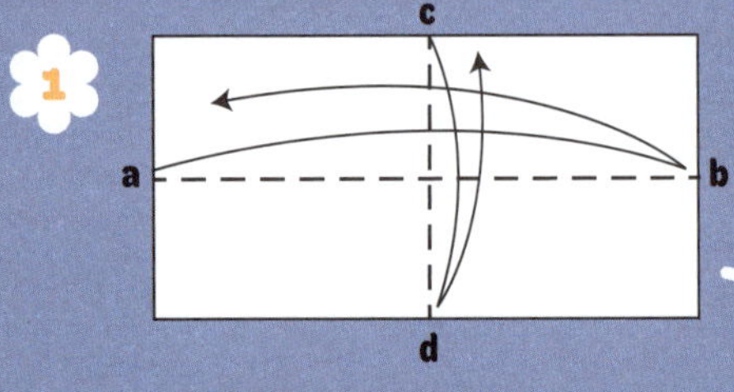

1. Cut a square in half. Set one half aside—you only need one. With the white side toward you, fold edge a to edge b, crease, and unfold. Repeat with edges c and d.

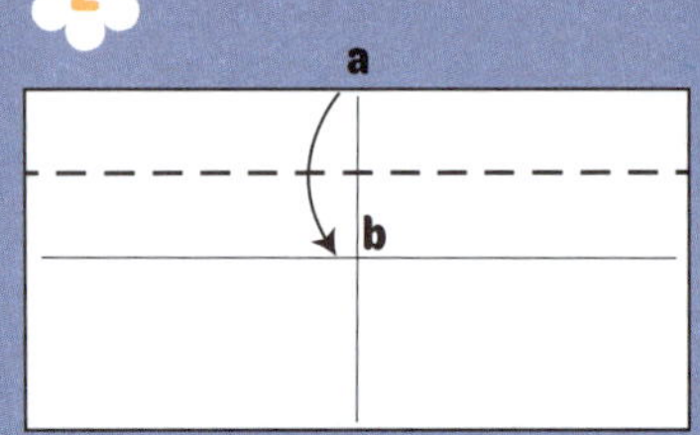

2. Fold edge a to point b at the center.

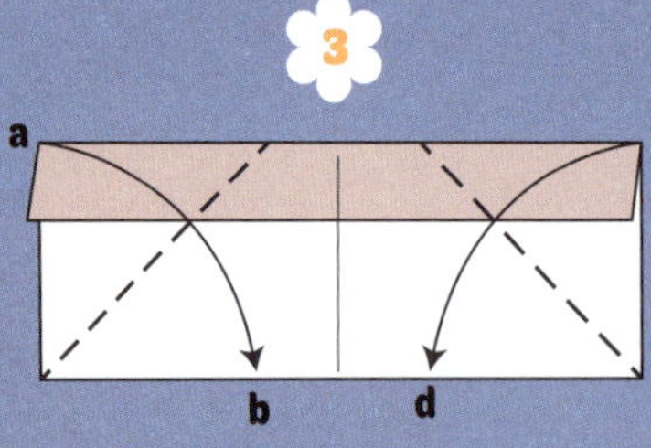

3. Fold point a to point b to create a triangle. Repeat with points c and d. Turn over.

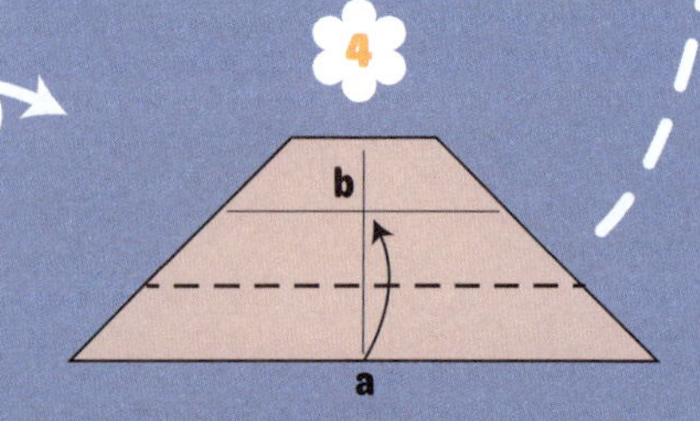

4. Fold edge a up to point b at the crease line.

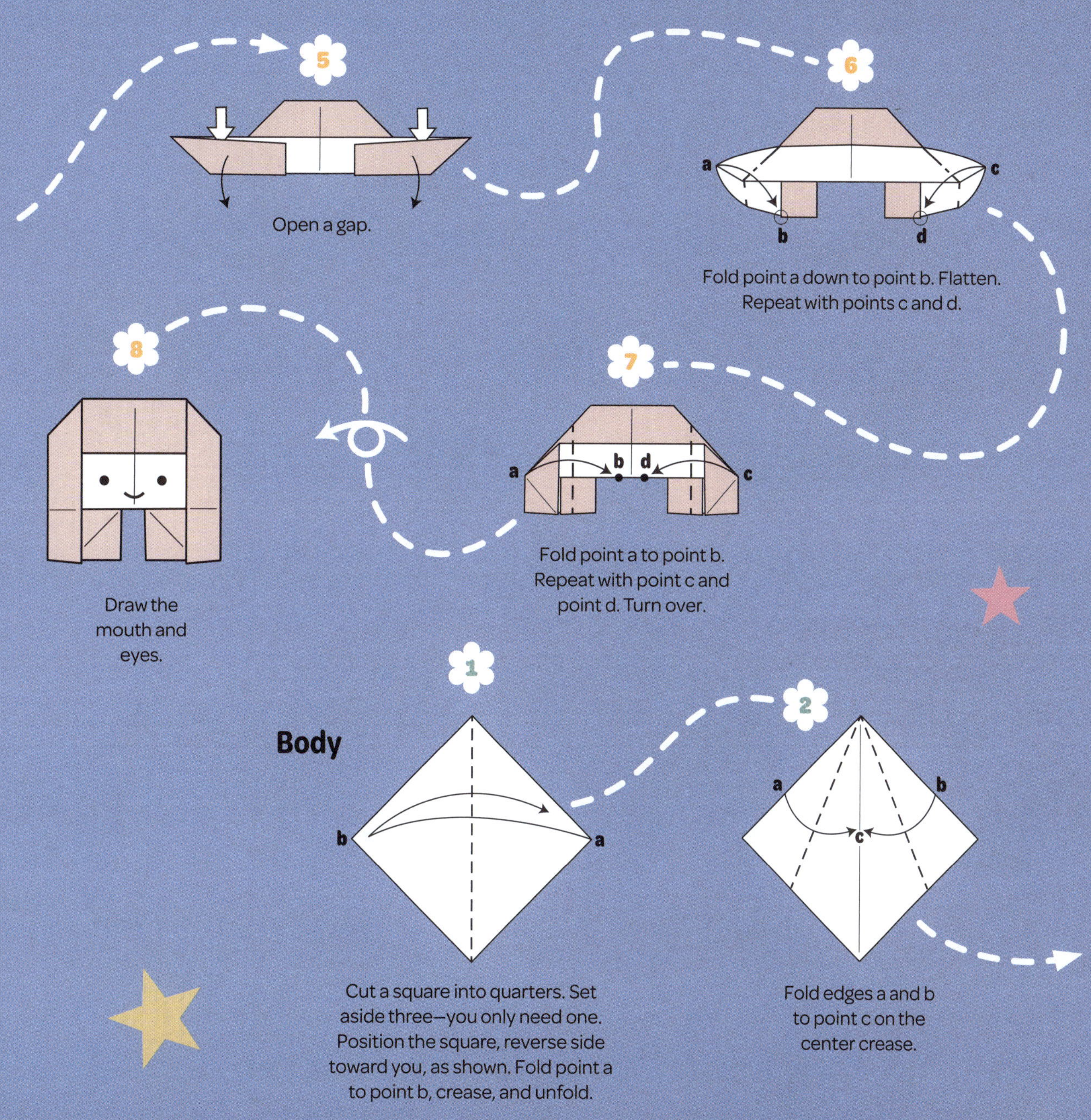
5
Open a gap.
6
a
c
b
d
Fold point a down to point b. Flatten. Repeat with points c and d.
8
Draw the mouth and eyes.
7
a
b
d
c
Fold point a to point b. Repeat with point c and point d. Turn over.
1
Body
b
a
Cut a square into quarters. Set aside three—you only need one. Position the square, reverse side toward you, as shown. Fold point a to point b, crease, and unfold.
2
a
b
c
Fold edges a and b to point c on the center crease.

Fold point a to point b. Turn over.

For a rectangular body, fold points a and b behind to the center crease. All done!

Assemble

To attach the short-haired or bob-hair head to the body, secure with glue or tape on the reverse.

For the long-haired head, insert the top point of the body into the gap between the hair. Secure with glue or tape on the reverse.

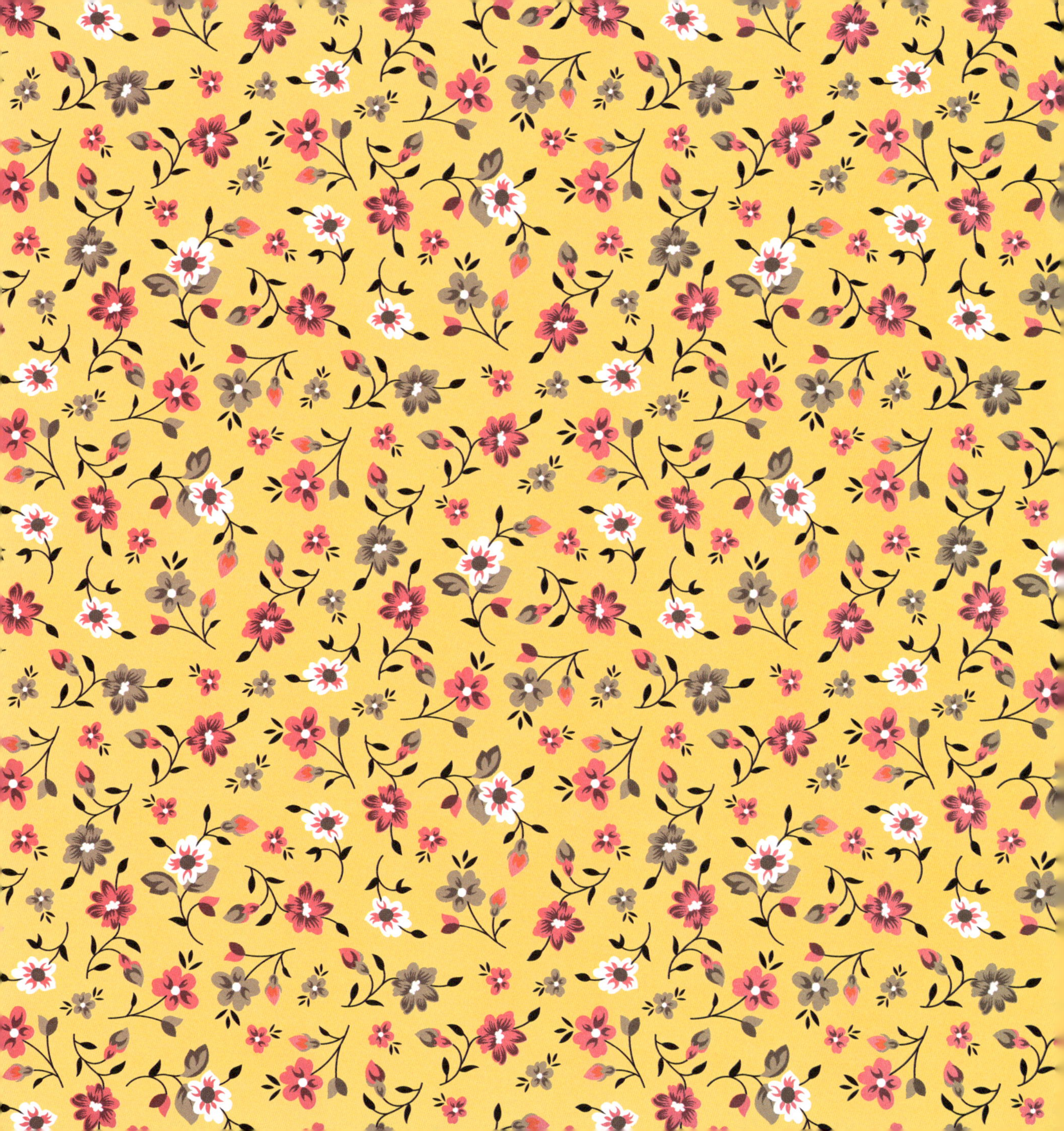

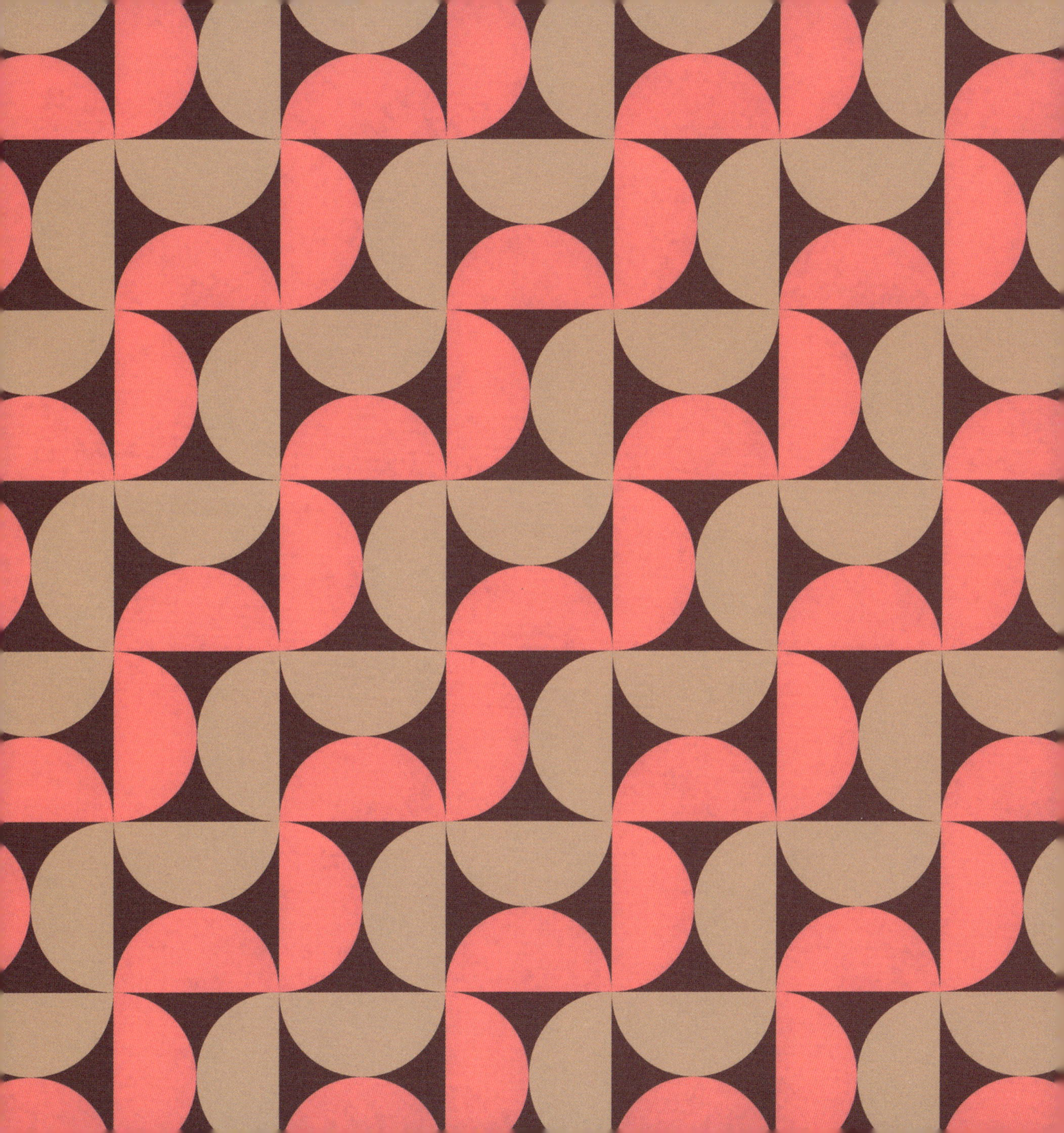

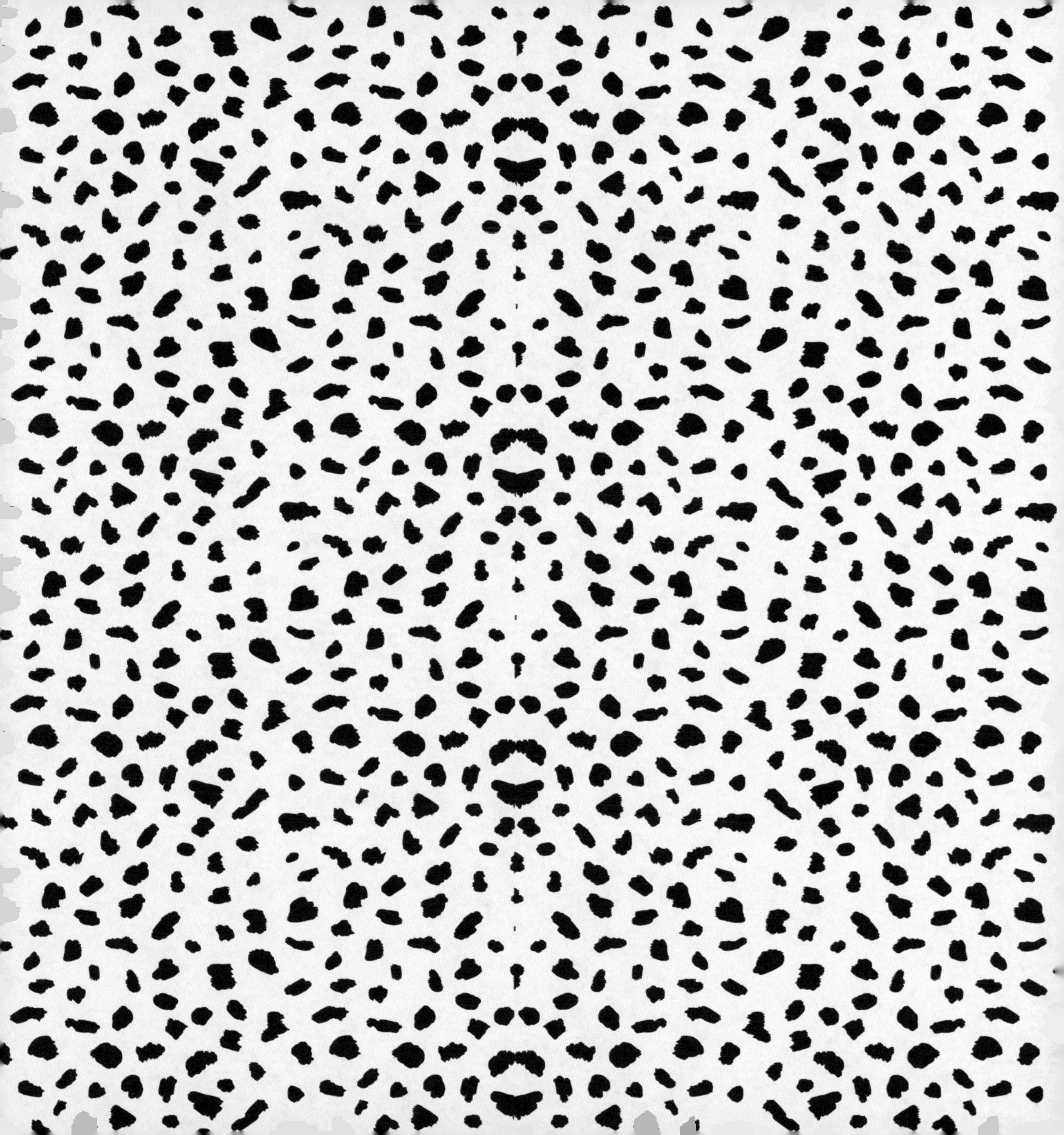

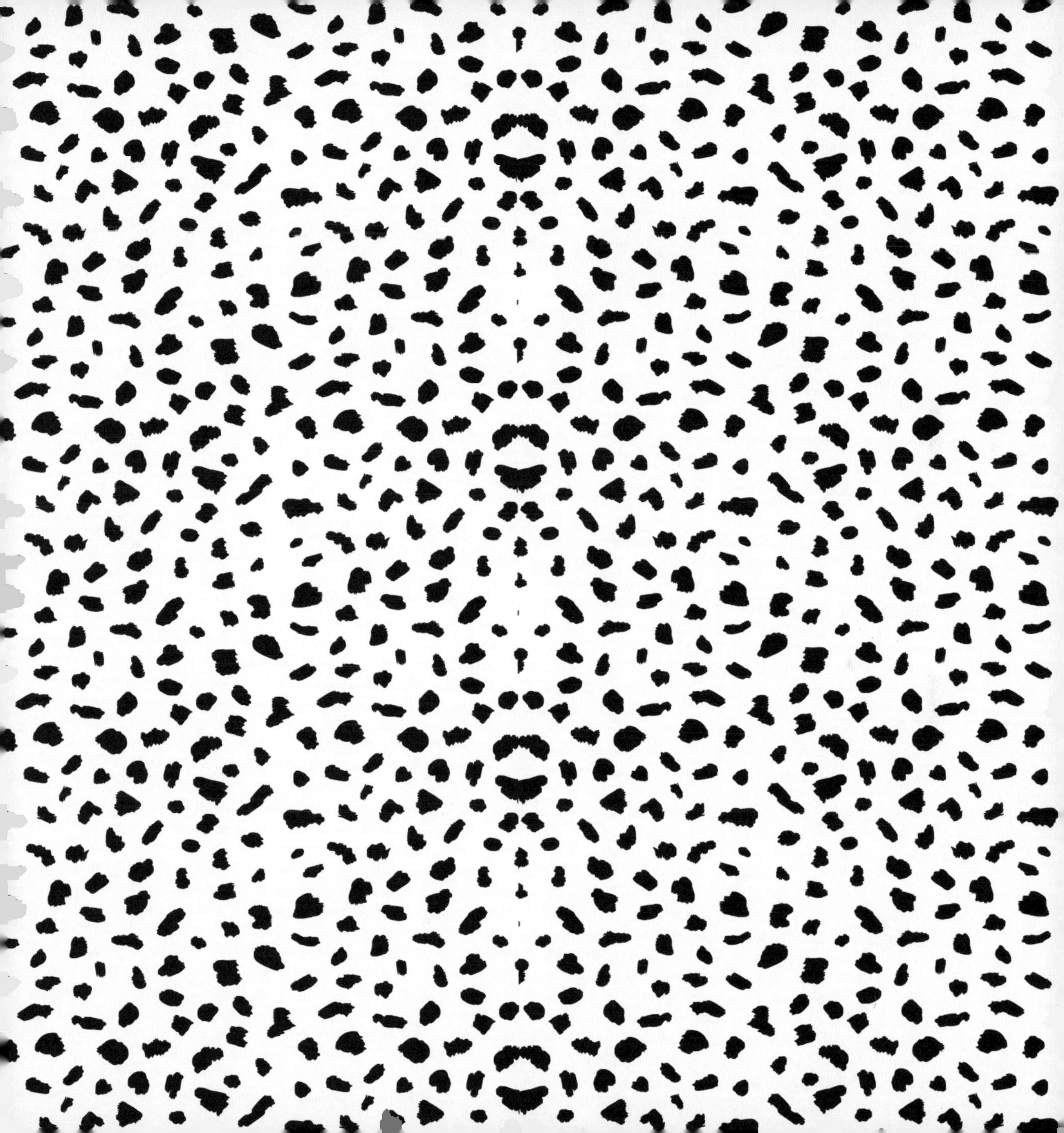